A SCHEME OF ECONOMIC THEORY

A SCHEME OF ECONOMIC THEORY

BY

G. L. S. SHACKLE

Brunner Professor of Economic Science in the University of Liverpool

CAMBRIDGE

AT THE UNIVERSITY PRESS

1968

CAMBRIDGE UNIVERSITY PRESS
Cambridge, New York, Melbourne, Madrid, Cape Town, Singapore,
São Paulo, Delhi, Dubai, Tokyo, Mexico City

Cambridge University Press
The Edinburgh Building, Cambridge CB2 8RU, UK

Published in the United States of America by Cambridge University Press, New York

www.cambridge.org
Information on this title: www.cambridge.org/9780521147552

First published 1965
Reprinted 1968
First paperback printing 2010

A catalogue record for this publication is available from the British Library

Library of Congress Catalogue Card Number: 65-14346

ISBN 978-0-521-06280-0 Hardback
ISBN 978-0-521-14755-2 Paperback

THIS BOOK IS DEDICATED TO

JOHN COHEN
RAFFAELLO MAGGI

CONTENTS

PREFACE

Men have sometimes supposed that they could exhibit the essential nature of economic society, and every important element and relationship in its structure, by a single unified model. Such was notably the case in the last decade of the nineteenth century and the first of the twentieth, when the combination of a subjective value theory with the analytic tools of the differential calculus seemed to uncover the *general* principle that bound together all valuations, actions and policies, and made of the whole an organism whose parts were manifestly interdependent and mutually determined. This splendid conception has been overlaid by the subsequent attempts to explain those problems upon which it was silent or plainly mistaken. Perfect competition can no longer be taken as the usual state of affairs; utility is at best only indirectly measurable; in a world of uncertainty, scarcity is not a guarantee of full employment; in a world where saving and investment are divorced from each other by money, the inducement to invest must be separately studied, and may depend on the growth of demand, so that the precarious coherence of growth-rates of output and investment must be examined. All these untidy accretions on the slopes of the acropolis obscure the beauty and symmetry of the neo-classical temple, and 'general equilibrium' is a description of a different world from the one which we observe.

No doubt economists are struggling for a new synthesis. The study of growth of wealth has replaced the study of the efficient use of given wealth. Yet still, in an explosively changing world, we have a fragmented economics. There are theories, one for this problem, one for that, but no general theory of society, even of economic society. One reason for this goes deep. It is the lack of a philosophical basis for economic theory. Economic life is looked upon as deliberative action, and again it is looked upon as action determined by the combination of tastes and circumstances. Which is it? Can it be both? Nobody asks, and such problems being unrecognized, the diversity of hidden assumptions creates a babel of conflicting languages.

I do not myself believe in the practicability or efficiency of a general model of economic society, embracing all its important aspects. Economics has lost its youthful innocence and simple creed, and now we have to be content with a variety of manuals of instruction, one for each kind of phenomenon. Yet we cannot be content to shuffle these around at random. If we cannot have a general model, can we not have a general scheme, showing how theories stand in relation to each other and what differences in their respective assumptions account for their different directions of attack? What general idea can provide a principle for such classification? If we claim that a basic semantic uncertainty is part of our trouble, ought we not to seek amongst the most fundamental notions for our guidance? Action, conduct, history: all these imply *time*, veiled, complex and elusive in its conjectural being but at any rate inescapable. I propose in this book to order theories according to their emphasis or otherwise on one or other of the meanings that seem to be bound up in the word *time*. Some of these theories are difficult, and as a secondary purpose I have had in mind the service I might render to some readers by dissecting these theories and giving a critical explanation and commentary on them.

I have sought throughout to be, in two senses, elementary. I have tried, that is, to find some basis for theory in the general human experience of life, to get down to foundations; and I have tried to take the only defensible stand of a scholar: understanding and knowledge must be sought with simple-minded unpretentiousness, casting aside, so far as at all practicable, any conventional armour of jargon or esotericism.

G. L. S. SHACKLE

28 September 1963

ACKNOWLEDGEMENTS

In the midst of all his preoccupations as Vice-Chancellor of the University of Lancaster and as Editor of the *Economic Journal*, Professor C. F. Carter with an incomparable kindness read this book in manuscript. I have referred in footnotes to some of his criticisms, and in response to one of them I have added a longer passage at the end of Chapter VI. If, despite his warnings, I have left errors uncorrected, they are of course my sole responsibility.

I wish to record the great debt I owe to Mrs E. C. Harris for the endless patience and care she has devoted to yet one more manuscript of mine, in typing, proof-reading and supervision of detail, in a manner quite beyond praise.

G. L. S. S.

7 November 1964

CHAPTER I

INTRODUCTION

Thought-constructions which are meant to show us order in the general scene of human action are bound to involve the ideas which we group under the heading *time*. These ideas are extremely diverse in outward form, in origin and psychic nature, and in the uses to which we put them. Some are the scholar's huge extension of our experience of momentary life into an infinite stretch of past and future, where our immediate sense of movement is made the basis of continuous narrative having a meaning and existence of its own outside that of a momentum or posture which our mind and its ideas conserve into each fresh present. Some are mere pieces of the scientist's algebraic machine, pure symbols of an abstract logic. Some are the best images we can give ourselves of certain vital elements of psychic life and consciousness. The present is in a sense the whole of life, embracing all that *is*. Within this present, the solitary moment of actuality, we call up mental pictures of 'the past' and we imagine possible experiences and actions which compose some one out of a limitless number of conceivable 'futures'. There are myths and comfortable or convenient or indispensable figments (so to call them without disrespect, meaning merely that they are inventions of our own and not self-evident 'facts' of nature) for which our time-ideas must find a place. Such ideas are cause and effect; the cumulative results which suggest duration; the 'remoteness' of imagined future events and the 'quantity of time' which we look upon as available for attaining some specified state of affairs; the degree to which sequential states seem condensed or squeezed together in a 'high-speed' process, or spaced out in a low-speed one; the basic idea of earlier and later, of chronological sequence. This great richness and diversity to be found within the skein of time-ideas has its powerful and commanding influence on the shape of our theories or models of action. For each aspect of time, and even for the total exclusion of time in every aspect, we can have a model which takes advantage of that particular conception of time to relate to each other in some meaningful structure the origins, directions, forms, phases and consequences of human deliberative conduct; and which has a special nature apt to that particular time-conception and rendered possible by it. The ideal would be a general model or sort of 'theatre of explanation' in which this or that part of the total illuminative equipment could be switched on for this or that particular purpose of analysis. Unfortunately such an idea has in practice little coherence, for it is as though only one bank of lights, or only a single spotlight, could be switched on at a time. It is only by a synthesis effected outside the formal logical properties of our various models, that we can achieve the effect of a total illumination of the field of human action from all directions. We cannot build up a general, omni-competent model by fitting together our special models, because it happens in many cases that one of these special models depends on assumptions incompatible with those required by another. Instead we have to strive for an insight which fuses informally and, if you like, non-logically, a number of strands which, in their formal aspects, mutually repel each other.

Doublethink of a sort may lie at the root of human nature. We feel ourselves to exercise 'free' choice. Do we mean uncaused choice? In what sense is choice free, if it is the mere response of given propensities to given circumstances? Yet if choice is more than such completely analysable response, if it has some element of strict *ex nihilo* origination and spontaneity, how can we hope to show that conduct is reason in action and that there is order in the human as well as the non-human scene? In the absence of such order, what reliance can I place on achieving by considered policy and action the ends that I desire? Yet all of economic theory rests on the view that conduct is a rational response to data. If such dualisms and basic incompatibilities belong to the very nature of human beings and human conscious life, it is plain that the models we use to explain that life will have to exhibit a corresponding unresolvable diversity. All we can do is to remain so far as possible in control of our thoughts, by clearly distinguishing from each other our different models and relating them to each other in a definite, explicit scheme. The formulation and justification of such a scheme, and the placing of various accepted models within it, are the purposes of this book.

The scheme we shall adopt arrays models according to their degree of involvement, first in the constructed, abstract, extensive time of the historian, the physicist or the economist concerned with growth and cycles of prosperity; secondly with that time which is directly known in experience, the time of actuality *in* which we feel, think, decide and act, the present moment, solitary, all-embracing, existing by its self-change into a different present; and thirdly with that *imagination* of extensive time which is a mental act necessarily taking place in the present moment and forming part of the experience and substance of that moment, but labelled with calendar dates other than that of the present and thus including the acts of expectation or of memory. What is the distinction between the first and third of these meanings of 'time'? It lies in the detached quasi-omniscience of the outside observer who constructs models or narratives in which numbers of distinct calendar dates are for him co-valid, all of them on an equal footing of reality and certainty, all of them, paradoxically, 'objective' despite the fact that the whole model or narrative is his own construct. How different this is from that continual creation of hypotheses about the possible outcomes of this available act and that, in the urgent, crucial and dramatic act of decision. The meaningful contrast is between time for the participant, time experienced or looked forward to, time seen from an 'inside' view, on the one hand, and on the other, time for the observer, time constructed from an 'outside' viewpoint and seen as a series of co-valid dates or moments. Many possible pairs of names suggest themselves as a means of marking this distinction. We could refer to interior and exterior time, or to constructed time and imagined time, or to narrative and expectational time (the distinction here being not between past and future but between description in an indicative mood and an activity of search in the interrogative mood). Perhaps the phrase *mechanical time* best conveys the idea of happenings treated as fact, and as in one sense sequential, but also as co-valid and capable of being all simultaneously viewed, analysed and stated, and treated as one whole, by a detached, non-participant observer. We shall refer to mechanical time and contrast it with expectational time. These two entirely distinct notions can serve as labels for the axes of a Cartesian diagram, or as labels for the respective series of rows and of columns in a square array or matrix. We thus obtain a scheme of double ranking or cross-classification in which models can be ordered according to their degree of involvement in time-concepts of one sort or the other. At one extreme of both rankings we shall place a thought construction which offers no footing for any kind of time-ideas except what is implied in the word 'action'. In this general equilibrium model all action is, in effect, simultaneous and involves no extensions of either mechanical or expectational time, the latter indeed being meaningless in the general equilibrium context. Midway on both rankings we shall place what we shall venture to call Marshall's time-spectrum, and beside it the sequence-analysis or period analysis of the Stockholm school. In each of these constructions, one so rich, realistic, fluid and difficult to hold in a clear focus, the other so carefully articulated, so much more artificial, abstract, clear-cut and precise, we find the detailed observer moving from point to point of his field of investigation, recording the contents of his acting subjects' minds at one date, their subsequent experiences and their revision of their expectations in the light of those experiences. Here we have both expectational and mechanical time, though neither Marshall nor the Stockholm school places in the forefront the uncertainty which is central to the concept of expectational time. It is on account of this relative neglect that we shall place at least an 'empty box' at a still more extreme position on the expectational time axis, in order to suggest the need for a theory of decision in face of uncertainty, that is, of *non-empty* decision. Beyond the 'expectational' ranking of Marshall and the neo-Wicksellians we shall place Keynes. His attitude to the dilemma of cause and choice is not easy to determine: we do not know whether he regarded expectations as ultimately inexplicable, or only as determined by too complex, subtle, elusive and unstable a collection of influences to be treated as a dependent variable within a self-contained economic model. His formal construction, in the main body of his work, left them as a law to themselves. Only in Chapter 22 of the *General Theory*, containing his brilliant sketch of the business cycle, Keynes allows expectations to be dominated by some fairly simple and discernible features of the business situation itself, and is thus able to describe a Marshallian cadence of events in which each phase visibly generates the next. The *General Theory of Employment, Interest and Money* is the most paradoxical of books. Constructed on a purely static and equilibrium frame of formal argument, it clothes this frame in a rich and suggestive mantle of ideas about expectations and their precarious basis and extreme unstable sensitiveness to 'the news'. In the present book I have had to find a special term to indicate this quality of Keynes's thought, and I have called his method *kaleido-static*. The patterns in the kaleidoscope change abruptly to something totally different, yet, given the exact character of the twist imparted to the instrument, these patterns have no doubt their own internal logic. Keynes saw in the business world a succession of highly unstable equilibria. In his formal construction he described the equilibrium of each situation, in his powerful gloss upon this formal argument he explained their almost explosive instability. The image of leaping cataracts, with pools of stillness in between, which is suggested to me by the *General Theory*, or the analogy with the kaleidoscope already proposed, are far from the deterministic, mechanical, cyclical and above all *self-contained* models which sprouted in such profusion in the fertile seed-bed of Keynes's work. The first to build a business cycle theory out of Keynesian elements was Sir Roy Harrod. Like Keynes, he preferred the freedom and accommodating generalness of a non self-contained model, receptive of any kind of stimulus from outside itself and responding in an appropriate and broadly reliable manner to each different kind, but not containing any *perpetuum mobile* of its own, to those in which a lagged interdependence of all variables could explain an unending and genuinely cyclical fluctuation. But Kalecki, Kaldor, Samuelson and Hicks have in succession opted for a 'business cycle machine' complete in itself, to which regular and therefore predictable oscillation is as natural as the tides or the seasons. These latter models give no place at all to expectation and have no use for expectational time, but exemplify in the purest form the concept of a historical pattern seen 'from without' by a detached observer in whose mind it exists as a simultaneously valid whole. These, therefore, lie at the extreme of the 'mechanical time' ranking.

Lastly our scheme includes something which is a model of thinking procedure rather than of the economic world itself. By arranging a list of headings as the names both of the rows and of the columns of a square array, and filling each of the pigeon-holes thus obtained with an entry specifying some type of relation between the pair of headings which give its 'address' in the whole array, we can gain insight into an astonishing range of different subject matter. The entries or elements of the square array or square matrix can be correlation coefficients or the parameters of linear equations or the technically-determined ratios between inputs and outputs in a process of production or the values of goods passing between nations in international trade or the outcomes of the confrontation of two particular strategies by two opponents in a game, and doubtless an unending list of other things as well. The beauty and simplicity of this scheme are well shown in its use by Leontief to analyse the structure of technical dependence amongst industries. In the Leontief model the explicit technical structure implies a latent time-structure which we shall compare with that underlying the Austrian theory of capital.

The meanings of time which give to each of our thought-constructs or models its special power of illuminating some one side of things, serve also as our principle for ordering or organizing these models into a general scheme. The purpose of such a scheme and principle is basically a semantic one, a search for insight into the meaning rather than the mere form or performance of each model. Merely to state a model's formal properties gives us no understanding of its fitness or unfitness as a tool of practical interpretation of those 'real' external human and social affairs in which each of us swims for his life; it gives no sufficient criterion of beauty, which must, to fulfil the deepest needs of the intellect, mean something beyond, though including, that mathematical elegance which all logicians instinctively desire; it does not tell us whether a given model is powerful, able to explain immense ranges of diverse phenomena as illustrations of a single thought. To judge these things we need to identify or contrast each property of a model with something in our own experience and in our genuine, unselfconscious pragmatic assumptions about what our world is and means. We need to secure from each model its answer to some root questions about the nature of things: all-pervasive completely interlocking cause and effect, a pure determinism; or history-making choice? Explanation of human actions and their turbulent conflux in the social stream of existence from an exterior and detached or an interior and participant viewpoint? Time as an extension or quasi-space, or time as the ever-solitary momentary locus of endless illusions of movement? Our semantic purpose goes further, however, than to question and explicate, as far as may be, the time-involvements of economic theory. The meaning of its time-involvement lies at the heart of an economic theory's most general meaning, but it is this general meaning itself that we wish briefly to survey.

Our title refers to models, and these self-sufficient constructs, each giving its own special interpretation of human business affairs as a whole, are the principal elements of our scheme of economic theory. The meaning of that scheme consists in the ordering of these models according to a basic idea, their time-involvement. But these models are themselves composed of more basic, more unitary and more general concepts than themselves; in particular, those of mathematics. The relation of the sciences of human nature and action to the vast mathematical tautology is disputable. There is a natural disposition and temptation to think that we can do for politics and economics, and even for art, literature and music, and for history in the most inclusive sense, what we hope to do for physics and chemistry and perhaps for genetics and the evolution of life-forms, namely, to present an incontestably self-contained and self-sufficient picture of inevitable necessity; to demonstrate that things could not be other than they are. If this is true of history, of human action, then it is plain that all our talk of choice, judgement and decision is empty vapouring, and our study of these things totally illusive. Yet order and reason are indispensable to understanding. If the cosmos provides men with a field of purposeful, and sometimes successful, action, offering a game partly of skill as well as of chance, there must be discernible regularities and repetitive patterns in the sequence of its states. If so, mathematics, the ideal and quintessence of reason, must be one of our chief resources.

If it be true that mathematics has evolved out of the empiric solutions of the practical needs of scientists and technologists, economists also have possibly fruitful difficulties to contribute. There are some superficially humble questions to which algebraists and analysts in their textbooks seem to give little attention, but which for economists are practical and pressing. Such is the need for a clear rule on the use of the two signs of equality. Equality is for the economist, in the exigencies of practical thought and argument, the name of two quite distinct and different groups of ideas, one of which can be further broken down into separate headings. First he wishes to distinguish circumstantial, conditional, casual and destructible equality from those kinds of equality which, for some particular argument or context, are permanent and indestructible. The price per unit of two distinct commodities, for example, can be equal or unequal, or the price asked by sellers and the price offered by buyers for one and the same commodity at some one moment may be equal or unequal. Here plainly we have circumstantial or casual equality, equality which can prevail or not prevail. The total money value paid by the buyers in some market on some day, and the total money value received by the sellers in that market on that day, can on the other hand be nothing but equal. This truistical equality is a trivial type of a more general notion, that of identical equality, under which we can discern a number of distinct situations.

Two algebraic expressions can be such that whatever set of numerical values was assigned to their unknowns the numerical values of these expressions would be the same, because one expression is merely an expansion or simplification of the other; or a symbol can be stated to be a mere shorthand for some function, whose numerical value, known or unknown, it therefore always has; or we can deliberately assume that a symbol which has some independent reference or 'content' of its own in some concrete context is equal, throughout some specified and limited range of circumstances, to some stable function of another variable; or we can stipulate that the 'independent' variable or variables in some function shall be confined to such values that the value of the function retains some specified constant value. To the economist it seems plain that these meanings of equality all stand in contradistinction to that kind of equality which is a special state or circumstance of a world which can, in the nature of things and even within the stipulations of a theory, a calculation or a proof, be in some other state or circumstance. He thinks of this second meaning of equality as exemplified by his concept of market equilibrium, and he is tempted to mark the distinction between equilibrium equality and all the other kinds of equality by using for all of the latter the three-barred symbol $\equiv$ instead of the two barred. Past crudities of argument which he may thus avoid are more serious than any offence against mathematical etiquette. Nevertheless it may be better still for the mathematician to devise a more discriminating notation, and have a separate symbol for each of the different types of non-frangible equality.

Mathematics in all its branches and developments, existing and still to be invented, offers an inexhaustible hope of finding new tools and methods of thought apt to the economist's needs. The immensity and richness of the field, far beyond the capacity of any one man to master in a lifetime, confronts us with a serious problem and danger. For economists who have stumbled on, or deliberately sought, some esoteric line of mathematical virtuosity may exploit it to powerful, but almost private, effect, since few others will care to master the technique for rewards which they cannot judge in advance. It seems plain that economists should be content with familiar mathematical tools until the inadequacy of these for some particular class of problems is proved. Two such methods can nowadays be considered a part of the fabric of economic thought, but despite their familiarity they still challenge the economist to be completely clear how the mathematical and the economic meanings are to be matched and interpreted into each other. The differential and integral calculus in particular is so perfect a vehicle for the economist's assumption that all economic conduct can be explained as the endeavour to maximize or to minimize something, that its methods constitute a positive danger of mistaking formal solutions for genuine insights. One purpose of this book is to suggest how we can seek to avoid such dangers by a very careful use of language. We have tried everywhere to make the step from subject-matter to logical manipulation an explicit and conscious one.

Matrix algebra, even considered merely as a shorthand vehicle for arguments which can be presented in other forms, is irresistibly appealing to anyone with a sense of the aesthetics of notation. We shall do no more than support this view by examples which show the square array itself, independently of all manipulation, as a *tour de force* of self-explanatory schematization.

APPENDIX TO CHAPTER I

A NOTE ON THE INTERPRETATION OF SOME CONCEPTS

In writing this book, the author has had in mind his own scheme of interpretation of some basic ideas. These hints of the meaning and structural connections of mathematical terms make, as will be seen, no pretence of being full or formal definitions. They are intended for the mathematically unsophisticated reader, and seek to suggest the immediacy and naturalness with which these abstract notions apply themselves to the description of economic models:

(1) *Measurables* (or *subject-matters*): each defines a class of circumstances in which measurement can be made, stating what characteristic of what kind of objects is to be measured.

(2) *Variables* or *classes of* (actual or conceivable) *measurements*, the class being defined by its subject-matter.

(3) A *value* of a variable is a particular measurement belonging to some class of measurements.

(4) A *vector* is a set of values, one from each of some list of variables.

(5) A class of such vectors formed according to some rule which restricts the allowable sets of values is a *function*.

The elements (measurements) composing a vector can be as many as we please, and consequently a function can be a rule concerned with as many variables as we please. If the function embraces only two variables, the equation which states the rule involved may be, for example,

$$y = 2x + 3.$$

Then if the value of the variable x (the particular measurement which, in some particular instance, represents the class of measurements called x) is given, the value of y can also be determined by performing the indicated operations, viz. multiplying the given value of x by 2 and adding 3 to the result. The function thus *restricts* us to those vectors (x, y) in which y is 3 more than twice x. *And so on*, in infinite variety of forms. In many cases the class of the vectors allowed by the function can be represented by a smooth curve (2 variables) or surface (3 variables). Then each particular vector or set of values is a *point* on the curve or surface.

CHAPTER II

EQUILIBRIUM

2.1. *Simultaneous choice*

Choice is *rational* when it conforms to a perfect knowledge of all circumstances which will affect its relevant outcome. We suppose that choice is aimed at securing a state of mind in the chooser, and those parts of the outcome of choice are in our sense relevant which affect his state of mind. Any gap in his knowledge of those circumstances destroys the possibility of his demonstrating to himself a rigid connection between his chosen act and his desired state of mind, and thus leaves his choice arbitrary. Amongst the circumstances which affect the outcome of any person's act are the simultaneous and subsequent acts of others. If he could wait until all these acts of others were performed, or at least irrevocably chosen, he could conceivably have knowledge of them and so choose his own act rationally. But it is not logically possible for each person to wait, before choosing his own act, until all others have performed or irrevocably chosen their acts. We can suppose, for the sake of argument, that only the immediate acts of each person will affect those parts of the outcomes of the acts of others which are relevant for those persons. Future acts being thus excluded from consideration, we are left with a set of immediate and therefore simultaneous acts, one for each person. Is it logically possible for each person to have knowledge of the simultaneous acts of all others in choosing his own? Equilibrium is a focal idea in economic theory because it enables us to answer Yes to this question.

Equilibrium is thus a means by which all persons in choosing their acts can be supposed to have equal and perfect relevant knowledge and equal freedom. Given a list of the persons, besides himself, composing the society, and given for each of these persons a list of all the acts possible to that person, each person can be supposed to draw up a list of all the distinct combinations of acts, one or other of which combinations will constitute the circumstances surrounding his own act. For each of these combinations he can be supposed to specify the act that he himself would choose, in case he were assured that the combination in question would prevail. The conditional promises, one for each person, thus derived, can now be supposed to be treated as a system to be simultaneously solved. A solution, if one exists, will be such as to prescribe for each person the act which is his own choice for that set of circumstances consisting in the performance by each other person of the act which the solution prescribes for that other person. Thus the solution is a set of acts, one for each person, such that each person would prefer the act thus assigned to him to all other acts open to him, given the acts thus assigned to all the other people. In such a solution, no one would wish to change his choice of act, for he would know that to do so would induce changes in other people's acts which would worsen his own situation: the solution affords him the best total combination of acts, including his own, on which universal free agreement can be secured. Thus the equilibrium thought-scheme or conceptual arrangement makes it logically possible to suppose that each person knows everything about the circumstances of his act that bears upon its outcome and ought, therefore, to bear upon his choice of it; and in cases where a solution exists, it makes each person's act fully explainable as the response which, all relevant circumstances being known to him, he is logically bound to make to these circumstances if his desires are to be as fully satisfied as these circumstances allow.

A model is in a sense like a skeletal map which shows only the short-cuts between a few selected places. The equilibrium model of rational human action, which we have described in a rather strict but also rather general form, shows such short cuts very strikingly. Two of the most radical of these short cuts are concerned with its treatment of time. For in the first place, people do not confine their actions to particular moments when all of them have exchanged conditional promises and solved the resulting system to discover for each of them his appropriate action. At any rate, they do not do anything like this consciously, even in regard to that class of actions which have to do with earning and spending income, or with establishing, equipping and managing, businesses. Whether, nevertheless, there exists any means or arrangement by which they can get information approximating to what would be available from the type of general pooling of conditional promises that we have imagined, is another matter which we shall soon discuss. This first short cut is a discrepancy between what people do do and what our model supposes them to do. It is conceivable, none the less, that people might do what our model supposes. Our second short cut is more serious.

The equilibrium model is here being presented as a solution of a problem in epistemics, the problem of how the knowledge needed as a basis of the choice of action can be acquired. In stating the model we explicitly dispensed with the future, saying that our universe of discourse consisted only of immediate acts, and that the outcomes of these, so far as relevant for their respective choosers, were unaffected by future acts. Yet in experience the meaning that any act of my own has for me depends on what I assume concerning the future acts of myself, other people and nature at large, perhaps to the end of my own lifetime and beyond. It is plain that any full study of the problem of how the necessary knowledge for rational action could conceivably be acquired, would have to consider how future acts could be known. And this problem, in our context, has by its nature no solution. For the idea that two or more persons, with rival or conflicting interests, can in general have perfect foresight is self-contradictory, unless we assume a complete determinism. But to assume determinism is to abolish the reality of the act of choice. So long as it claims to show how choice of action can be rational, our equilibrium model, in any form simple enough for demonstration, sets aside a basic, inherent circumstance of human life, indispensable even to the idea of consciousness, the circumstance of our ignorance of the future. Even the most elaborate and far-fetched scheme for the pooling of conditional promises could not elicit them from people yet unborn.

In this second short-cut the equilibrium model, strictly understood, pays a high price for its cutting of a Gordian knot and its incisive elegant simplicity. Yet it is so greatly illuminating, in its general conception and especially in the refinement of its economic application which we shall soon examine, that it may still seem worth studying. To reconcile ourselves to this price we have, at any rate, three distinct expedients. We can suppose that the members of the society resign themselves to a total ignorance of the future and therefore disregard it: this is to turn the enemy's sword upon himself, and claim that if taking a view of the future is too difficult a thing to analyse, it is too difficult to practise. Or we can suppose that the members of the society are wholly engrossed in living from hand to mouth, so that their acts and choices are concerned purely with securing food and fuel for immediate use. Or lastly we can suppose that the future with all its mistiness and uncertainty of detail is looked on, so far as immediate acts are concerned, as part of an essentially constant environment of choice, just as the British winter climate governs the buying of clothes in the autumn despite our knowing nothing of each future day's particular weather.

To give us our bearings in the landscape of economic understanding as a whole, such thoughts are useful, but they should not be allowed at first to blur the outlines of the problem of timeless rational choice which the equilibrium model, considered in detachment from 'realistic' preoccupations, is plainly apt for. That problem will be seen in its purest essentials if we eschew all compromise and simply expunge from our argument the whole complex of ideas which 'time' connotes. It may be asked whether logically we can do this. We are concerned with actions, even if only the psychic actions of thought and resolve, and do not actions 'take time'? Our answer is a paradox: in the sense of the question, our model has all the time in the world, for we are concerned with actions each of which is neither preceded nor followed, in any effective sense, by any other action. Thus these actions are not embedded in any history, and there is really, within our model, no means of measuring the length of a time interval. The 'time' required for the actions we are studying thus has neither length nor location, and it is simplest to say that ours is a timeless model. The same conclusion can be reached by a different approach. The question that our model serves to answer is: Given the tastes and the resources of each person in the society, and given that each has a complete knowledge of the circumstances relevant to any action of his own, including the associated actions of other people, what will his action be? In this formulation of the problem, there is really no reference to any sequence of events, nor to any duration, nor to any aspect of time whatever. Since the terms of the question call for no consideration of time nor make any mention of it, neither need the solution do so. We are in a timeless world.

2.2. *The market as a* knowledge *exchange*

The actions which concern economics are those of making things more useful for sustaining or enjoying life, exchanging them and getting the usefulness out of them. Remembering that our model contains only the immediate future, allowing each person to choose just one act and to choose it in view of its direct and immediate effects only (there being no time, within the model, for any later effects) we can condense to a very simple statement the effect of other people's actions upon his choice, for these actions will affect him only through the quantities of needed goods that he can get from the other people, the prices at which he can get any specified quantities, the quantities of his own goods that they will buy from him and the prices at which they will buy any specified quantities. Now the idea of conditional intentions and a mechanism for pooling and solving them as a system suddenly takes on a concrete form, that of the open and perfect market where each good can be bought and sold at a price which is the same for all buyers and all sellers, and which equalizes in total quantity the conditional intentions to buy with the conditional intentions to sell. At each hypothetical price of each good, each member of the society will have in mind the particular quantity he would buy or sell at that price. If it should be the case that a higher price is associated for everyone with a smaller quantity bought or a larger quantity sold, there is likely to be one price which balances or equilibrates, in terms of quantity, the desires to buy and the desires to sell. In the language of our general statement of the meaning of equilibrium as a scheme allowing rational choice, each act is an act of buying or selling; the range of different acts is a range of different quantities, of this good or that, which would be bought or sold; and the condition which will select from among possible acts the actual one, is the price of the good. The vehicle of information, the means by which this economic-equilibrium model solves the problem of how the necessary knowledge for rational action can be supposed to be available to each member of the society, is *market price*, which, by the meaning we give to the word 'market', is declaratory, public and uniform. Esoteric as the start of our discussion may have seemed, we have now brought it round to something commonplace. Markets and prices are a means to information, to providing a man with a basis of judgement as to what best to do.

Thus described and illustrated, equilibrium is a mere receptacle needing to be filled up with the answers to many questions of interpretation and detail, of possible modifications or even of exchange for different lines of thought, and of facts about applicability and consonance with aspects of the observed world. Such questions are: Under what conditions will a solution exist? In the market illustration, what guarantee is there that price will be able to adjust to each other the quantities demanded and supplied? Upon what circumstances does its efficiency in this direction depend? What illumination of real experience is gained by investigating so rarified a model? Can this model be adapted to contain aspects of time without disastrous loss of simplicity? Does an equilibrium of exchange require, or allow, the idea of money? In what sense, or under what conditions, does an equilibrium represent an optimum?

2.3. *Relaxations and extensions*

We have set out the notion of equilibrium as a formal answer to the question whether circumstances and arrangements are logically conceivable, in which a number of people, whose actions will *together* form an environment determining the outcome of each such act, can none the less each choose his own act with full relevant knowledge of its outcome. The tastes or preferences of each member of the society, the quantity he possesses of this means of action or that, the technical character and possibilities residing in these means, can be stated as equations, and the total system of these equations can be studied to discover whether a solution prescribing compatible acts, one for each person such that, given the acts prescribed for others, he will prefer it to any other, exists; or whether there are many such solutions, or an infinity of them, or none. In constructing this model, our suppositions have been extremely stringent and artificial. We have now to consider whether it can be modified, or essentially embodied in some larger frame, so as to help us answer further and different questions.

In a brilliant article, Professor Hayek defined equilibrium as a situation where the *plans* of all the members of the society were compatible with each other up to some nearer or more remote future date or 'horizon', in the sense that no plan entertained by one member postulated actions on the part of another, or included beliefs about the behaviour of 'nature', which did not form part of the plan of that other. The interval between the 'present moment' when the Hayekian equilibrium exists, and the horizon, may be looked on as a sort of extended 'moment' when all that occurs is the direct outcome of the intentions held at the beginning of that interval. Within the interval, there is neither need nor possibility of new ideas or for *decisions*, there is no need for thought, and in so far as a 'plan' differs from an 'intended action', it does so merely in its degree of complexity.

The simultaneity of all the actions which compose our model makes it needless, as we have shown, to consider duration. Our model being an exchange economy, these actions consist in parting with or receiving certain objects which can most typically be thought of as quantities of perfectly divisible goods; of goods, that is, which can be parcelled out with as fine a difference of size as we like between any two parcels. To dispense with duration is to change the *dimension* of the quantities with which ordinary descriptions of an economic process are concerned. Thus *output*, *income*, *expenditure*, *consumption*, *saving*, *investment*, are all of them names of quantities belonging to the class of *flows*, that is, quantities expressed as so-and-so many units of mass, volume, value, etc., *per unit of time*. Since we have so far had no use for units of time, we have had no need to distinguish between quantities held or possessed at an instant, and quantities handed over or received at an instant. But one obvious direction in which we might be tempted to try to make our model more superficially realistic is to adapt it to the notion of flows, by considering an indefinite sequence of identical 'moments', within each of which the events would be precisely those determined by an equilibrium just as if this moment were the solitary whole of our timeless model. We have to ask whether anything is gained by such an adaptation.

The stationary state is designed to remove from equilibrium the blemish of its refusal to consider time as extension, without sacrificing its advantage of studying only a single state of affairs. It requires us, therefore, to think of time as something which can have a sort of length, and can in a familiar way be represented geometrically by a straight line as though it were one dimension of the 'space' of our senses of sight and touch. This extension can be divided into equal intervals or 'days', and each such interval looked on as the locus of a set of actions bound together in the same way as those of the timeless system, but able to be thought of as the exchange of such and such quantities of goods *per* (unit) *interval*. In the timeless system this set of actions takes its precise character from the tastes, circumstances and endowments of the members of the society. Their tastes we regard as an integral part of their respective selves, and thus in an extended instead of a timeless model we can take these tastes as naturally unchanging. Their endowments, in the timeless model, consist of certain quantities of exchangeable goods. In the extended model, however, the goods received must be supposed to be used up and destroyed in the process of extracting their usefulness from them; and those parted with must be replaced by goods freshly produced with certain resources of personal strength and skill, portions of nature such as physical land, and so on, and it is the quantity or effectiveness of each of these resources which must now be assumed constant. But in the extended system there is a further matter to consider. Not only physical endowments and tastes, but also *beliefs*, knowledge, expectations, might in general be supposed to be carried from one interval to another, and these must be supposed not merely to be constant but to be such as to lead to the same actions in the next interval as in the present one. If tools or stocks of commodities are preserved from one 'day' to the next the very same quantities must be carried forward from that next day to the one beyond, and so on, else the circumstances of the individual and hence his actions. will be different. In short, he must not learn or forget or exercise imagination, he must not be positively thrifty or unthrifty, he must live each day, in effect, from hand to mouth just as though each day was in fact an isolated, time-solitary self-contained world. The intervals or 'days' of the stationary state are a string of identical beads and anything we can learn from all the beads we can learn from any one of them. It is thus pointless to suppose that there is any 'carry over' of goods from one day to the next and if, for the sake of being able to speak of flows of goods at a time-rate of such and such a quantity per day, instead of simple isolated acts of exchange, we insist on envisaging the stationary state, we may nevertheless just as well deem it to consist of perfectly self-contained and non-communicating days. And this view has a certain advantage.

If we insist on such realism as the stationary state has to offer in comparison with the timeless system, this realism will perhaps make a special appeal when we wish to consider change. For change is something which can only occur to a persisting entity. We may wish to ask what will happen to a given stationary state, which exists as a response to certain circumstances surrounding the society, when there occurs an abrupt jump carrying the society to a new, but thereafter persisting, set of circumstances. Some natural disaster or technical discovery might alter 'overnight' the situation of the people. In such a case, if we have supposed their 'days' to be self-contained, their response can be simple and immediate. But if we have supposed that they carry over goods from one day to the next, the amounts of this carry-over will be different, in general, in the new circumstances and the adjustment from one pattern of carry-over to another will be complicated and even threatens to prevent indefinitely the settling-down to a new equilibrium.

In fact, however, in a *comparative statics* analysis which such a once-over change would typify, it is better to be ruthless in our assumptions just as it is in studying a single state of affairs. Comparative statics does not consist essentially in the study of change itself, as an event, for our purposes are best served when we reduce this event to a mere formal shift of our own attention from one state of affairs to another. It consists essentially in the comparison of two distinct states of affairs, and whether these states are the successive states of a persisting society or the concomitant states of two distinct societies, or whether indeed there is any specified temporal relationship between them at all, is beside the point. To study change in itself for the sake of understanding its mechanism is something entirely different with which comparative statics has nothing to do.

We have referred to the question of the conditions in which an equilibrium solution will, in the mathematician's sense, *exist*, which means whether such a set of actions, one for each member of society, is logically possible, whether it can occur and is not rendered illusory by an internal self-contradiction. But there is another question. Even when the conditions for the existence of an equilibrium are fulfilled, how can this solution be found out, how can the equilibrium *come* into existence? This further problem is sometimes called that of *stability*, for it is assumed that we have a stationary state which is thrown out of its even stride by some event from without, and the question then is whether and by what path it will find some new equilibrium.

If, for the new 'external' circumstances, which may include for example the sets of resources, or the technical knowledge, respectively possessed by this and that member of the society, a new equilibrium exists, it has none the less somehow got to be identified. The two questions, whether or not a solution exists, and how it can be discovered, are different in nature. One is a matter of pure logic or mathematical proof, and it is the *certainty* of the answer, if it can be given at all, which has conferred upon the notion of equilibrium its unique prestige. The other question is one to which the theoretician is entitled to offer countless suggestions amongst which the choice, so far as logic is concerned, is arbitrary, because we have not made, and have at present no observational basis for making, sufficient assumptions about the process of diffusion of knowledge.

Even in the special case of the exchange economy we have to ask by what process of diffusion of information throughout the society we can suppose everyone to find out what prices in the market would result from this or that action of his own. We can nowadays, of course, suppose that all conditional promises to buy or sell, expressed as equations, are fed into an electronic computer and that the members of the society simply accept and obey its instructions. But for the sake of realism it is often thought desirable to describe a more conventional market process which feels its way by a succession of provisional, non-binding bids towards the equilibrium set of prices, those which will equalize for every good the quantity which buyers desire, at the established price, to buy, and that which sellers desire at that price to sell. The idea of such a process of 'tâtonnements' as Walras called it, or of re-contract as conceived by Edgeworth, does not at all conflict with our requirement of essential timelessness, provided we can guarantee an eventual arrival at the same solution as a computer would obtain. For it is only the final equilibrium commitments which are to be simultaneous, in the sense that there is to be no opting out, no revision in the light of further knowledge. Our second question, beyond that of the existence of equilibrium, is whether such a process would lead to the discovery of the equilibrium solution, or whether the members of the society would be perpetually misled and baffled by the provisional effects of their own bids into altering those bids by too great or small amounts. The strictest timeless equilibrium model, determined by solving a system of co-valid equations ('simultaneous' equations in the logical sense) does not leave room for this problem. And once we replace the notion of actual mathematical solution (for example, by a computer) by that of market processes, we are compelled to make some assumption as to how precisely these processes lead to a more and more coherent diffusion of knowledge and beliefs throughout the society, until equilibrium is attained. Any such assumption is drawn, we may say arbitrarily, from a host of possible assumptions, and these do not partake in any way of the logical security of equilibrium itself.

Before we try to sum these matters up by asking in what sense is equilibrium a tool of thought, there is one question which our timeless exchange model itself may raise. In this model we have spoken of a *numéraire*. Why not of money? The actions which are chosen in the equilibrium model, whether simple demands or offers of some good or whether complex schemes even involving the doing of one thing 'after' another, must all be chosen 'now', in the timeless simultaneity of commitment, and each must be chosen as a whole, else there can be no complete knowledge for the other members of the society. Equilibrium is action in equal freedom and in equal and (relevantly) perfect knowledge. It is in simultaneous complete commitment that the meaning and essence of equilibrium reside, it is for this that we require and stipulate, and thus that we define, its timelessness. In the equilibrium model there is no future, for the future essentially implies ignorance. (This by no means excludes Hayekian equilibrium, for the plans which must there be harmonized can each be considered as a crystallized whole, like a plan to erect a machine whose parts can only be assembled in one sequence.) If the actions are those of exchange, the goods exchanged must therefore be thought of as useful in themselves and desired for their own sake. But money is not such a good. Its usefulness and desiredness are derived ultimately from the belief that it will be exchangeable for other goods whose character need not be specified to himself by the owner of the money until the moment of exchange. Money is precisely that which enables choice to be deferred. But equilibrium is that model in which no aspect of choice can be deferred. Money, of course, serves also as a *numéraire*, as a unit of account, but this function is entirely distinct from its use as a store of value. To use a *numéraire* is to select one of the goods which are being exchanged for each other, and declare that the number of physical units of this good which exchanges, in equilibrium, for one physical unit of some other good, shall be called the price of that other good. Each good can have only one price, for the universal diffusion of complete (relevant) knowledge, which constitutes equilibrium, precludes any inconsistency of prices. Money, however, is a means of deferring choice, and as such has no place in a model of simultaneous, complete and final choice.

Why study equilibrium? Why investigate minutely the bearings and interpretation of an idea seemingly so artificial and remote from experience? This question may simply mean: Why have a theory at all? A theory or a model, as we sought to show, is intentionally and designedly phantasmal and is of set purpose constructed with only a minute percentage of the immense assortment of impressions that life supplies. If we do not care to see the wood, but are only interested in the trees, we need make no effort to select a viewpoint, to marshal the scene into a composition, to have some control over the army of observations or records. If we are content to gulp the stream of conscious life down without seeking in it any general structure or orderliness beyond its obvious small-scale stereotypes of action and effect which we recognize and use for living from minute to minute, we need no general theory. To seek insight is to theorize. But beyond this general challenge to theorizing itself, what of the efficacy, efficiency and value of this particular specimen of theory, the concept of equilibrium? Two main propositions together compose the case in its favour. First, it reveals coherence and single-mindedness in the complex conduct of the individual. He is seen by all of us to do all sorts of things with all sorts of means, materials and tools. Does this mean that he is aimless or hopelessly confused by distracting and conflicting stimuli or pressures? On the contrary, we are well convinced that he or she is seeking the maximum possible fulfilment of a unified plan of life, even if this plan is not explicit in the individual's mind. The measure as well as the nature of this fulfilment is a state of mind, but the degree to which this state is attained depends on a fine balance of technically diverse uses of basic resources limited in quantity. Equilibrium shows the action-chooser as endeavouring to 'get the most' out of his limited strength, skill and material possessions. He has a purpose and pursues it with the nearest approach to rationality which is open to him. Secondly, the equilibrium model makes the simplest and most natural assumption about the 'rules of the game' within which this attempt takes place, namely, that these rules are the same for all the players. It does not assume that these players all have equal strength and skill, equally ample and excellent equipment.

Equilibrium is a paradox, for in it each rival interest serves itself by offering advantages to all the others. These advantages consist essentially of knowledge, knowledge for each man of what alternative results he can attain for himself by this or that action of his own. He buys this knowledge about his own environment by contributing his own conditional promise to the general pool. Equilibrium is action subject to rules which ensure the essential communication. Because of these rules, freedom is not perfect, but because of them also, it is *equal*, and because of them, finally, *knowledge* is (relevantly) perfect and therefore also equal. Only endowment can be unequal, and the consequence of this possible inequality we shall consider below.

In the paradox of equilibrium the members of society, acting in equality of freedom each in pursuit of his own interest, yet compose a coherent whole. This coherence of action amongst uncoerced individuals arises from coherence of knowledge. Certain facts are public and correct and are taken account of by all individuals. When we confine ourselves to the economic model, this publicly available and general basis for choice consists in the prices of all goods, which prices signal to all members of society the fact and implications of particular conduct on the part of others. Upon this all-pervasive web of communication rests the most important single fact which economics has to convey, namely, the universal interdependence of the conduct of human beings: my conduct has, in however slight degree, consequences for everyone else, and what results I have the power to bring about depends upon what actions are chosen by others.

Equilibrium, as we have here interpreted this term, is the set of actions chosen by the members of the society in equal freedom and equal and perfect relevant knowledge. But these two equalities imply nothing as to tastes, capacities or means. How much a man possesses and how much he can enjoy whatever he possesses are questions not connected in any simple way with the questions of what he knows and whether the formal 'rules of the game' are identical for all people including himself. Thus what we have discerned as to the nature and meaning of equilibrium does not directly talk to us of *welfare* when that word is applied, legitimately or not, to the whole of the society. To complete our discussion of equilibrium we must make an excursion into so-called *welfare economics*.

If general equilibrium gives to each person the best that his circumstances allow, when we include in those circumstances the results of the equal freedom which it accords to every other person to strive for his best position; then it is natural to ask whether this equality of freedom and of knowledge, and this perfect adjustability of all elements, such as prices and quantities exchanged, which are the defining conditions and the necessary foundation of equilibrium, ensure in some sense an absolute best position for the people of the society all taken together? Though this question is natural, it cannot be answered until we have sorted out its implications. The solution, the specified set of actions for all the people of the economy, which in the timeless exchange economy means simply the quantities of some goods given up and of others received by each person, will be different if we start with a different initial situation, this initial situation consisting in the means of action possessed by person A, by person B and so on. It is natural that a different problem should have a different answer. Thus we have to ask whether one distribution of means of action, of goods initially possessed, is better than another. There may be sense in the statement that if *everybody* has larger means in position R than in position S, position R is better; though this statement ought really to be interpreted as meaning: 'No matter whom you ask, he will say that, for him, position R is better.' But we cannot make any sense of a claim that R is better because, although some people are worse off in R than in S, this fact is outweighed by the fact that others are better off. There is no meaning in a comparison between one person's happiness and another's. Let us not confuse this statement with another which is concerned with two possible states of happiness of *one and the same* person, who, therefore, is in a position to judge between them: 'Your happiness, when I see plain evidence of it, makes me happy. And thus if your evident happiness increases enough, this will more than make good a deterioration in the rest of my circumstances.' The latter statement involves only one person's judgement and preferences, and so it is meaningful and self-consistent. We can no more add together judgements made by different individuals, each, necessarily, from that individual's own, peculiar, special viewpoint and constructed with his own inimitable private, personal criteria, than we can make an intelligible perspective drawing, partly from one and partly from another viewpoint. When we ask whether situation R, in which each separate person has more goods than he has in situation S, is the better of the two, we can answer: 'Everyone thinks so.' But if we then go on to ask: 'Do they, then, all think the same?' the answer is that the question really means nothing.

CHAPTER III

MARSHALL AND THE MODES OF CHANGE: THE MARSHALLIAN TIME-SPECTRUM

Alfred Marshall's *Principles of Economics* strangely and touchingly exemplified its author's conception of how things happen in economics. The basis of that conception was the gradual, natural and rational adaptation of any economy's productive arrangements to its shifting needs and increasing knowledge. This process was thought of as occupying decades and even generations, yet as retaining its unity through time and the meaningful succession of its stages. Just so, the *Principles* evolved. The fresh, audacious beginning, the gradual blossoming, carrying the work to its peak, Mr Guillebaud tells us,* in the third edition, was followed, even as in the individual trees of Marshall's famous forest, by a loss of the vitality and beauty of youth. Yet the adaptation to pressures from critics and from events, and from the unrelenting perfectionism of a master mind, were inevitable and part of the scheme of intellectual Nature.

Marshall sought to understand the natural history of a society's business life. The ultimate sources of this life, from which flowed not only its pattern on any day or in any year, but the sequences which those patterns might show and the secular evolution of those sequences, had in them an essential constancy and permanence, for otherwise the investigator's probings would not have been science. But this constancy at the heart of things is little stressed. Marshall's supreme effort was to display the natural stages of the development and flowering of the business organism, whether firm, industry or nation, as a unity, as something orderly and understandable though requiring decades or generations. Hence his insistence on the distinct and differing effects produced by given forces,

* Marshall, *Principles of Economics*, Ninth (Variorum) Edition with annotations by C. W. Guillebaud (Macmillan and Co. for The Royal Economic Society, 1961). See Vol. II, p. 18.

according as these forces had a short or long time in which to work undisturbed; and hence his struggle to bring into a clear light his conception of the *normal*, the result that would have been achieved if, contrary to the facts of an ever-changing environment and the endless stream of 'accidents', this non-disturbance has been realized in truth.

By the *natural history* of a society we seek to suggest the complexity of the process whose nature Marshall sought to grasp. This was not a stationary process of endless identical repetition, for Marshall puts aside such a scheme as not really to his purpose. For him the real economic process, distinct both from the rigid stationary state and from the secular march of civilization, was the flow of events resulting from the release or discharge of given forces in a given environment. Forces thus coming suddenly into action, from a technical discovery or a shift of taste, produced events in distinguishable cadences, earlier and later, until in the end, if no more shocks arrived from without, the long landslide of adjustment brought about a fresh repose. By this model Marshall was enabled to perform a great *tour de force*, the use of the notion of equilibrium to describe, analyse and understand a sequence of events, a process of change. This is Marshall's most profound, daring and powerful innovation, his greatest claim to fame.

Equilibrium as a scheme of thought about economic society is unmatched in its efficiency. It binds together into a single whole (namely, the general equilibrium) every aspect of every person's and every firm's business affairs, displays all these distinct particulars as each governed in the scope of its action by all the others together, and thus offers a universal explanation of every act, every plan and every policy in the whole economy, showing them all as unconsciously contributing to a broadly sensible and desirable result. Equilibrium solves by a master-stroke the problem of how we can suppose that a great number of individuals, each deciding simultaneously with all the others upon his own act, can nevertheless choose that act in the light of all relevant knowledge of those acts of others. It does so by its key idea of the conditional promise or conditional intention, in which the extent of each act depends on some circumstance common to all the acts and itself determined by their combined effect. This circumstance is price, the number of units of one good which can be had or must be given in the market in exchange for one unit of another good. The web of markets and their prices, embracing all goods, transmits and balances in all directions the rival desires, within and between individual minds ringed about by scarcity and limited human knowledge, which determine how much of each good is annually produced and how this output is shared amongst users. This is the meaning of the ideal and ultimate general equilibrium. But the adjustments needed to attain it, from any given present situation which history has thrown up, where the material and organizational residue of past policies no longer reflects current desires, take time, some much and some little. The business society of employed and employers and self-employers, of earners, spenders and government, we may see as a unified flux preserving, like a river, a constant image despite the ceaseless change of its constituent waters, but also needing to be studied at different distances, as it were, from its source, that is, after different degrees of opportunity have been given for the splashing short-period torrent to become the 'deep silent strong stream'. (VI, (viii), § 10.)

Marshall does not explicitly pose, nor solve by the concept of conditional intention, the problem of how a set of simultaneous acts can all be rational when rationality means correct choice in the light of all relevant knowledge. Yet his whole account of business conduct shows this conduct as a constant search for better and better adjustment to the circumstances which the collectivity of individual courses of action creates for each individual. Marshall is always aware of the interdependence of all things in the economy, but his practical method of studying these things is to take them two at a time and hold the others still; to hold these other things still, first in one configuration and then another, choosing these successively assumed environments so that they compose an orderly and natural development. Marshall trains his spy-glass on one ship at a time, but he knows that it floats upon a world-wide ocean.

Marshall sought the permanent and the essential beneath the transitory appearances of things. The society which lay beneath his eye, Victorian Britain, was growing in population, wealth, knowledge, technical accomplishment, literacy and the breadth of suffrage. Its industrial methods and commercial arrangements were fast changing. Yet this rapid evolution, Marshall seems to assume, was explicable by some permanent logic of human existence. It was to this constant and fundamental something that he tried to reach down. Some of the procedures for doing so, that might readily suggest themselves, would have been against the spirit of his curiosity. If society manifested growth, fluctuation, fashion and friction, the explanation of all these was part of his objective and could by no means be assumed away without stultifying his whole enterprise. Yet they were only symptoms of an underlying physiology or basic constitution, and it was this, in its completeness, that he wished to study. This physiology could be studied, he thought, in the individual cell, the firm. Cells were, of course, widely diverse, yet they had a vital structure in common. There was a typical or representative cell, or firm, in which these common features were in balance, so that no one of them was masked by others; a cell which represented the greatest common divisor of all cells. Marshall wished, moreover, for something vivid, particular and concrete that could be described in detail, yet would give the clue to vast tracts of data, would *illustrate* the structure of economic society and the source of its unceasing self-renewal. Thus he invented the representative firm, a firm marching in the middle of the advancing army, conformist and unexceptional, yet alive.

'When demand and supply are spoken of in relation to one another, it is of course necessary that the markets to which they refer should be the same.' (V, (i), §2.) Supply is the number of natural or physical units of some commodity or service (some good) which in given circumstances will be offered in some market in some calendar interval. Marshall's effort is above all directed to elucidating the kinds of circumstance and their effect which can prevail in a market, and the effects which arise when the meaning of our expression *some calendar interval*, which we have invented as a vehicle for Marshall's thought, is assigned in various ways. The framework of time-ideas involved in the notion of the calendar interval comprises the date from which the person, whose conduct we are studying, looks at this interval; the time-distance separating this date from the beginning of the interval;

the length of the interval; and the location of all these things in the real historical context.

It would be meaningless to speak of a quantity demanded, or offered, without reference to the length of the time-interval between whose beginning and end this demand was to be filled or this offer made good. Supply and demand are essentially magnitudes of dimension xt^{-1}, where x stands for some number of natural, that is, physical, units and t stands for some number of units of time-lapse. Thus the mere measurement of supply requires the length of the relevant interval to be specified. But this length plays another part besides that of the denominator in a ratio of quantity to time-lapse. Given that ratio, the length of the interval directly measures the total amount of employment that will be given, in respect of that interval, to any equipment or industrial or commercial facilities, in the widest sense, that may be installed for the purpose of supplying the market; and also the amount of employment that will be afforded to any skilled workers or managers who may be trained and engaged for the same purpose. That is to say, if the interval in contemplation is a long one, the preparations which it will be worth while to make, with this interval solely in view, will be more elaborate, expensive and powerful in their cheapening effect on the product, than if only a short interval was in question. But a third question enters into the matter. The cost, and even the sheer technical possibility, of making elaborate productive preparations to supply some good within the beginning and end of some future interval, depend on the time-distance between the date when these preparations are begun, and the date of the beginning of the interval. The fact that supply is always and necessarily a time-rate of flow brings the notion of time-interval into our discussion in a purely technical way. It is the other two ideas which give Marshall's conception its special shape, and we may refer to them as the length and the futurity of the supply-interval.

One of the difficulties that Marshall presents to the casual reader of his book is that he does not explicitly distinguish between the length and the futurity, in the foregoing senses, of the supply-interval. He is content, instead, to speak of a short or long period in a sense which embraces both meanings.

One of our chief purposes in what follows will be to support this contention by quotation and to demonstrate that both meanings are implicit in his use of the word 'period'. Marshall's 'long period' is thus a period which makes it both *possible* and *profitable* to invest heavily in productive and commercial facilities, by allowing time for such facilities to be both constructed and used up.

Marshall's treatment of time may be set out in the following propositions:

(i) Choice amongst rival actions is made according to the *expected* outcome of this action and that. Marshall is not uniformly explicit, clear and precise; but he is quite explicit on so many occasions as to make his basic view unmistakable.

(ii) The individual can, however, be at fault in representing to himself now the satisfaction he would experience, on some future occasion, as a sequel to a given present course of action. He may, for example, underestimate the acuteness of the needs he will feel at some future time. His present choice of action will then differ from that corresponding to a perfect 'telescopic faculty'. His 'waiting' will be less than it ought, his contribution to the supply of capital smaller than would be good for him.

(iii) '. . . the *supply* of capital is controlled by the fact that, in order to accumulate it, men must act prospectively, . . . they must sacrifice the present to the future' [To the extent that they are willing to do so] 'the progress and diffusion of knowledge are constantly leading to the adoption of new processes and new machinery which economize human effort on condition that some of the effort is spent a good while before the attainment of the ultimate ends to which it is directed.' [Thus the *demand* for capital arises from the existence, and continual fresh recognition, of] '. . . new ways of economizing effort by expending it in anticipation of distant wants'.

(iv) New circumstances cannot modify planned conduct until they become known to the persons making these plans. The transmission and absorption of knowledge take time, and thus, for example, the influence of technical innovations or changes of fashion on demand may work their way only gradually through society.

(v) When a multitude of rival suppliers are offering perishable goods which are already in their hands, they can do nothing but accept the market price, since each would merely benefit his rivals by refusing it. In such a situation, each supplier can control neither his price nor his output, the latter being already determined as a historical fact. Demanders can, however, choose how much to buy at whatever price the market establishes. Marshall reads this type of situation as governed by demand.

(vi) The greater the futurity of the date when a given time-rate of delivery is to begin, the greater the freedom of a supplier to adjust his productive means for this purpose, and the lower the price per unit, in general, which he will be able to accept for a given daily or annual (etc.) number of units delivered.

(vii) The greater the length of time during which a given time-rate of delivery is to be maintained, the more far-reaching the preparations which will seem worth while for this purpose.

(viii) Since a very long prospective period during which delivery at a given time-rate (or average time-rate) is to be maintained necessarily means a remote futurity for the later parts of such a period, the two ideas of *futurity* and *large total volume of production* merge with each other. Marshall blends them into the conception of the 'long period', which thus allows the fullest possible assemblage and adaptation of all known means within the ultimate reach of the producer to be attained.

(ix) The concept of the 'normal' enables a static analysis to be applied to an ever-changing reality. This concept is, perhaps, the most difficult in all of Marshall's work. It represents the position which a producer (for example) could look forward to achieving if his preparations were able to take advantage of some stated futurity of the date when production was to begin, and of some stated minimum of total sales of the product after that date; and if he could ignore all possibilities both of more improvised and immediate production and sales, and of more carefully and lengthily prepared distant production and sales. Take, in other words, a named calendar interval, specified as to the location both of its beginning and its end in the real historical calendar, and also as to its futurity; and let the producer concentrate all his energies on the activities of that interval. Then his operations in that interval will approximate to some cross-section taken from that 'stationary state' which Marshall eschews as an analytical tool. All this is on the understanding, however, that all the rest of the economic environment has likewise taken this interval as its sole object of preparation.

(x) Yet this conception of the normal must be reconciled to the fact that no producer can have anything like a complete knowledge or picture of the possibilities that will open out as he traverses in practice the time-distance separating him from the named calendar interval for which we suppose him to be preparing. Even the 'normal', therefore, lacks purity and precision. As the business man goes on in actual deed and experience from the date when he made his plan towards the date when his output will first flow on to the market, he will recognize possibilities of 'internal economies of large scale' which he formerly perceived only dimly or not at all; and if the interval between making the plan and starting to sell output is a matter of years, he may enjoy the benefit of an industrial environment which has improved during this interval, and offers him, at its end, 'external economies' which he had not counted on. The scope and effect of this process of discovery cannot be specified by theory, and the concept of normal circumstances of supply must therefore remain in some degree vague.

(xi) Price depends on quantity and time. By time we mean in this statement Marshall's period, short or long, embracing within its own length both the futurity of the interval in which the goods are to be put on the market, and the length of that interval. By quantity we mean the total quantity, to be put on the market in the interval, of the goods whose unit price we are discussing. To the proposition which thus seeks to express Marshall's philosophy of supply price in six words, we should add something which is also, if less plainly, implied in Marshall's own account of things, namely, that price also depends on the historical context, that is, on the particular point of development which technology, business organization and the total social environment have reached. A firm's own discoveries and improvements, its internal economies, which emerge in the course of executing a production plan, are, for itself, amongst the most relevant aspects of the new environment which each passing year presents to it. Thus, we might say more elaborately, price depends on the quantity to be produced, the time available for producing it, and the specific historical starting point. Two things follow. First, at any given historical starting date, price being a function of two independent variables will require a surface, or at any rate a family of curves, for the expression of its dependence on these two variables. Marshall recognizes the possibility, rather than the necessity, of organizing one's thought on these lines, and then only in a footnote reference to a proposal of Sir H. Cunynghame to that effect. Secondly, every different starting date will require a new family of curves, and from this it follows that once a production plan has been actually carried out during a lapse of historical time, any fresh plan will necessarily have a different starting point and will accordingly need a fresh set of curves. Suppose, then, that after two equal periods in the first of which it produced a relatively small and in the second a relatively large quantity, the firm contemplates a third equal period in which it will revert to a small quantity. Its cost of production of this small output, Marshall says, will be less in the third than it was in the first period, for in contracting after its expansion the firm will not lose all the benefit of the economies it discovered and applied during its expansion. In Marshall's manner of expressing this we have another instance of his reliance on the common sense of his reader and of Marshall's own taste for short cuts of exposition which leave the step-by-step logician far behind. For Marshall draws us (V, (xiii), §2) a two-dimensional diagram of quantity plotted against cost, which nevertheless represents the expansion path through time of the firm. What has happened to the time-dimension? It has, of course, simply been telescoped into nothingness by the projection, upon some plane at right-angles to it, of the 'space-curve' (*anglice* 'twisted curve') which would be traced on a surface connecting unit cost with quantity and *historical* time. For in the very meaning of the 'time' whose dimension has thus been left for the reader to imagine, Marshall's impatient realism has again taken charge. This 'time' is both the abstract period, long or short, which is available to the firm for constructing and amortizing expensive equipment, and *also* the time of evolving techniques and of the actual march of history which carries the firm into a different environment. Supply-price, then, depends on quantity and on three meanings of time: the futurity, the length and the historical location of the interval in which the given quantity is to be produced. Marshall would never have dreamt of so tedious an articulation of his meaning. But his elliptical statements naturally confuse the pedantic reader.

(xii) '. . . the term "margin of production" has no significance for long periods in relation to commodities the cost of production of which diminishes with a gradual increase in the output: . . . in problems in which the tendency to increasing return is in effective force, there is no clearly defined marginal product.' (Appendix H, § 1.)

Whenever an increase of the total quantity produced per time-interval of given length requires an increase of the associated total expense of production, the modern economist would say that marginal product and marginal cost are definable, unless the extra product or the extra means of production required do not even approximate to continuous divisibility. Marshall continues: 'In such problems our units have to be larger. . . .' However, he is *not* here arguing from indivisibility to the non-availability of marginal analysis; on the contrary, he is arguing from some not clearly stated ground, to the non-applicability of marginal ideas and hence to the need for lumpish analysis.

In all this, Marshall's peculiar triumph is his creation of a unity out of the conceptions of equilibrium and of evolution. Equilibrium he conceives in a sophisticated, profoundly thought-out form where the economic subjects concerned are not helpless weights on elastic strings but anxiously thinking humans whose conduct is governed in part by their knowledge and the stages in which they attain it and by the conjectures which they base upon it. Equilibrium is a state of adjustment to circumstances, but it is a fiction, Marshall's own and declared fiction, for it is an adjustment that *would* be attained if the very endeavour to reach it did not reveal fresh possibilities, give fresh command of resources, and prepare the way for inevitable, natural, organic further change. It is this powerful conception which is the most worth-while object of study in Marshall, and it is to this that we shall confine ourselves in endeavouring by brief quotation and comment to justify our interpretation of his thought.

Despite some startling references to changes of human nature which had occurred within fifty years (Marshall wrote, after all, in the High Victorian era of optimism and belief in human 'perfectibility'), he clearly recognizes the dependence of science and understanding on some ultimate fundamental permanence:

that more fundamental substance of economic organization, which depends mainly on such wants and activities, such preferences and aversions as are found in man everywhere—they have a sufficient element of permanence and universality to enable them to be brought in some measure under general statements, whereby the experience of one time and one age may throw light on the difficulties of another. (App. C, §4.)

The balance amongst themselves which these basic and lasting forces achieved Marshall called the *normal.* This balance was not abstract, instantaneous and final, but a process of more and more deeply grounded adjustment, a steady and continuous settling down. The reality was the process, and if we elect to describe it as having 'stages', this is merely a concession to the limited powers of the human mind:

the problem of normal value belongs to economic Dynamics; all suggestions as to economic rest, of which the hypothesis of a Stationary state is the chief, are merely provisional, used only to illustrate particular steps in the argument, and to be thrown aside when that is done. (V, (v), §2 footnote.)

The fabric of Western thought is antique and inscrutable in its origins and built everywhere, however new its forms, with material salved and refashioned from earlier times. In recent centuries this continuity is strikingly illustrated by economics. Marshall finds the source of his own idea of the normal in Adam Smith:

that much quoted, and much misunderstood doctrine of Adam Smith—that the normal, or 'natural', value of a commodity is that which economic forces tend to bring about *in the long run.* It is the average which economic forces would bring about if the general conditions of life were stationary for a run of time long enough for them all to work out their full effect. (V, (iii), §6.)

However tiresome Marshall may be in the confusions and obscurities of his formal definitions, all is redeemed in the limpid blending of the concrete and the abstract in his examples. 'Normal' can refer to an immediate and ephemeral, or to a far-reaching and profound, adjustment; or to something between; how are these aspects, which form, as Marshall himself constantly insists, a continuous reality (Preface to First Edition, p. vii), to be kept separate? He shows it in the example of the 'scarcity of meat lasting a year or two' and the effect of this on the demand and supply of fish. It is done by casting over all irrelevancies the spell of *ceteris paribus*. Thus the hourly vagaries of the weather, along with such slow changes as that in 'the number of those who are brought up as seafaring men', are alike blotted from view, and '. . . the normal price for any given daily supply of fish is the price which will quickly call into the fishing trade capital and labour enough to obtain that supply in a day's fishing of average good fortune'. (V, (v), §4.)

Marshall is far from uniform in his wording and seems sometimes to deviate in thought as well as in expression from a single consistent line, but such a line is visible. The Marshallian period, whether short or long, is something seen by the business man *ex ante*, it is something whose circumstances must be estimated and planned for in advance, and we may understand Marshall most easily by treating all his comparisons, whether so described or not, as comparisons of alternative *plans*. The length of the period which such plans envisage is, as Marshall constantly insists, a continuous variable, ranging from a day to several generations: but between the extremes of this range, and even between interior values, the differences between the relevant plans are so great as to be qualitative, and can best be studied in the guise of types, the market period, the short period, the long period: 'As regards *market* prices, Supply is taken to mean the stock of the commodity in question which is on hand, or at all events "in sight".' (V, (v), §8.)

In a brilliant passage (V, (iii), §1), Marshall has shown how, by means of future markets, expectations of future grain supplies and demands affect current prices. Crops which can be estimated with some confidence and accuracy because they are already growing are what he means by 'stocks which are in sight'.

As regards short periods—the supply of specialized skill and ability, of suitable machinery and other material capital, and of the appropriate industrial organization has not time to be fully adapted to demand; but the producers have to adjust their supply to demand as best they can with the appliances already at their disposal.

Marshall was far less interested in the short period than in the long; for modern writers on the contrary the short period has been the main object of study, for one respectable and one less honourable reason. They are doubtless right in thinking that the business man seldom plans ahead for more than a few years, recognizing the futility and even the dangers of attempting it. But there is also the need of the perfect competition hypothesis for a rising supply curve to intersect a horizontal 'demand curve facing the firm'. Without it, there would be nothing to limit the growth of the individual firm until it had swallowed the industry and turned competition into monopoly. Thus there is a possibility that perfect competition in the long period is an untenable hypothesis: for the rising supply curve depends on some factor or factors of production being fixed in quantity, and it is the absence of any such fixity which is the essence of the long period. Marshall was acutely aware of this dilemma and furnished the essential clue for modern solutions of it. (V, (xii), §2; V, (xv), §4.)

It was in the long period that Marshall sought the arcanum, the real nature and meaning of the economic process as a part of the historical process. But in his long period we can distinguish two separate aspects or modes of treatment. It can still be truly said that his essential view is forward-looking, his business man's standpoint is the *ex ante* one. Now, however, besides the plan devised at the very beginning, we are shown the inevitable subsequent need to revise this plan, or at least to fill in with newly attainable detail the blanks which at the beginning were deliberately left in it. The precise forms which economies of scale must take do not become visible until the firm actually approaches that scale. The business man will learn all the time from his experience. Moreover, the possibilities which will open before the firm will depend on the discoveries, developments and innovations of other firms. Thus in its rounded reality, Marshall's long period is not merely a panorama from the mountain pass but an actual journey down the valley. The need to follow the stages of this journey, to allow the business man to take up new viewpoints and make new plans is obvious. Yet in this realism Marshall has exposed himself to a charge of confusion, for, save in one passage, he fails to make a clear distinction between a curve visualized by the business man at one moment and looking to one other moment, at which production on this or that scale can begin; and a curve which traces the firm's actual growth path through an infinity of moments between two given dates. Each of these conceptions is referred to as 'the long period curve'. Marshall had good reason for discussing both types of curve, but not for treating these two utterly distinct ideas as though they were the same. Before we illustrate this matter, however, we must dispose of the simple concept of a curve relating price to annual output when the *start* of that output is being planned for a long time ahead, and when (equally important) the output itself is counted on to continue for many years. From the quotations which immediately follow we can draw evidence on the meaning of *long period* in its pure *ex ante* sense:

For short periods people take the stock of appliances for production as practically fixed; and they are governed by their expectations of demand in considering how actively they shall set themselves to work those appliances. In long periods they set themselves to adjust the flow of these appliances to their expectations of demand for the goods which the appliances help to produce. (V, (v) §5.)

Thus that investment of capital in a trade, on which the price of the commodity produced by it depends in the long run, is governed by estimates on the one hand of the outgoings required to build up and to work a representative firm, and on the other of the incomings spread over a long period of time, to be got by such a price. (V, (v) §7.)

This second passage is almost the only one to be found in the *Principles* which clearly indicates the *double* condition required of a 'long period', viz. that it should contain a first sub-period long enough to make the production of equipment *technically* possible (e.g. long enough to permit the actual laying of brick upon brick to build a factory) and a second, and much longer, sub-period, starting after the completion of the factory, long enough for the factory to earn its first cost in the form of (discounted) quasi-rents, that is, differences between the sale proceeds of its product and the cost of its collaborating factors and materials. As always, it is in his examples that Marshall is most vivid and appealing:

In the case, for instance, of an order for a single locomotive, the question of readjusting the plant to demand would hardly arise: the main question would be whether more work could conveniently be got out of the existing plant. But in view of an order for a large number of locomotives to be delivered gradually over a series of years, some extension of plant 'specially' made for the purpose, and therefore truly to be regarded as prime marginal costs would almost certainly be carefully considered.

'Gradually over a number of years': Why is the supply-price per unit of the product a decreasing function of the durability of plant capable of a given annual output of the product? Because durability increases the number of units of product which the plant can be expected to produce during its life, and thus reduces the prospective contribution required from each unit towards the first cost of the plant. Or we may say, at a given price per unit, a given quantity of the product must be spread over many future years in order that a small enough quantity of extra plant shall be able to produce it. We come now to our strangest item, where in a footnote typically more incisive than the text, Marshall seems almost to concede that a family of supply curves, each referring to one and only one set of simultaneously valid conditions, might have better served his purpose than the strange hybrid of alternatives and consecutives on which he sustains the bulk of his explanation:

A rise or fall of the demand or supply price involves of course a rise or fall of the demand or supply curve. If the change is gradual, the supply curve will assume in succession a series of positions, each of which is a little below the preceding one; and in this way we might have represented the effects of that gradual improvement of industrial organization which arises from an increase in the scale of production, and which we have represented by assigning to it an influence upon the supply price for long-period curves. In an ingenious paper privately printed by Sir H. Cunynghame, a suggestion is made, which seems to come in effect to proposing that a long-period supply curve should be regarded as in some manner representing a series of short-period curves; each of these curves would assume throughout its whole length that development of industrial organization which properly belongs to the scale of production represented by the distance from [the vertical axis] of the point in which that curve cuts the long-period supply curve. (V, (xiii), § 1.)

Had Marshall considered the matter still a little further, it might have occurred to him to give his long-period curve a clearer meaning by *deriving* it from Sir H. Cunynghame's family of short-period curves. Each of the latter must be assigned a different futurity, since each pre-supposes a different development of industrial organization. Each of them, in fact, expresses purely the connection between price and output with a *given* organization and equipment. Thus these Cunynghame curves could be disposed in echelon each at right-angles to a futurity axis, and each could then be intersected by the estimated demand curve of its own date. The points of intersection could then be projected on a plane at right angles to the time axis, and would thus indicate the expected expansion path (price-output path) of the industry.

The object of Marshall's life-long study, the phenomenon he strove to understand and to describe in the eventual 858 pages of a book which took twenty years to write and thirty to revise, belongs to no ready-made pigeon-hole of a conventional classification. This object was the flux of fact, the patiently observed reality of evolving Victorian business life. Analysis must suppose something constant and permanent at the heart of things, but in economics this essence manifests itself in a ceaseless development. For other writers economics has meant pure logic or simple historiography. It was the endeavour to cut a small segment out of history and display its structure as a time-consuming logical pattern that makes Marshall's method sometimes seem obscure. His tools were as personal and special as his task. Some of these tools are serviceable only in Marshall's own hands, but his division of supply conditions into three types or periods has proved indispensable to his successors.

CHAPTER IV

KEYNESIAN KALEIDO-STATICS

4.1. *Keynesian kaleido-statics*

To treat the state of affairs existing at some date, or the events of a very short interval ending at that date, as composing something coherent in itself, is to use the equilibrium method. The only relations considered and accounted for are those subsisting between quantities which can adjust themselves instantaneously to the conceptions existing in the minds of business men and other action-takers. Relations between quantities which can respond only slowly, or not at all, to manipulation are left outside the analysis, and these quantities are looked on as composing a given environment or 'receptacle' within which adjustment of the fluid quantities to each other and to the given environment takes place. Some of the quantities composing the total picture are flows, quantities of dimension XT^{-1}, and a lapse of time may accumulate such a flow into a stock, of dimension X, which will constitute a new element in the 'fixed' or 'given' environment of the later date. Such slow evolution of the scene may conform to the conceptions existing in the minds of some, or all, action-takers at the earlier date, when the lapse of time begins. However, there is another mode of change by which one momentary scene can be transformed into another, and that is by an abrupt alteration of one or more of the environmental quantities, or of the conceptions in the minds of business men concerning these environmental quantities as they are or as they will be; and indeed it is the action-takers' notions which matter, for these notions, rather than the 'objective' quantities themselves, are the basis of choices of action. According to this cataclysmic mode of change, the history of the economy will be made up of alternating periods of analysable equilibrium and of non-analysable landslide movement towards a new equilibrium, after the old environing circumstances have been thrown into a new pattern.

Such is Keynes's method in *The General Theory of Employment,*

Interest and Money. It is the unmistakable Marshallian tool used with a heightened contrast between the precise, formal and explicit analysis of equilibrium and the mere outline and suggestion of the rumbling and tumbling cascade which leads from one equilibrium to another. There are two other, and more essential, differences between the Marshallian and the Keynesian version of this tool. Keynes applied it to the economy as a whole, not, however, by a vast proliferation of micro-economic variables, bringing on the stage a crowd of individual earners, consumers, employers and so forth, but by aggregating the economic doings of the members of each of these classes and treating each aggregate as a single whole. Thus Keynes initiated *aggregative* or *macro*-economics. This, even if faintly foreshadowed by business cycle theories and by Quesnay's *Tableau Economique*, was a masterstroke for which he has received too little credit. Secondly, Keynes drew out one glittering strand from the Marshallian skein of rather prosaically bundled-up ideas and showed it to be the live conductor of the impulses that mattered: the *General Theory* is founded on the idea of expectations and their precarious and trembling balance even in what is formally equilibrium. Marshall refers again and again to entrepreneurs being moved to this course or that by what they expect, but he nowhere treats expectations as an active and untamable source of disturbance.

There is an arresting contrast between the method and the meaning of Keynes's book. The method is the analysis of equilibrium, the endeavour to account for men's actions as a rational, calculated and logically justifiable response to circumstances which in all relevant essentials they thoroughly know. The meaning is that such rationality is in the nature of things impossible and baseless, because men confront an unknown and unknowable future. When with the painful labour of years he had set out his theory of employment in that detailed and carefully articulated form which academic acceptance requires, and being challenged on this or that aspect of these details, he replied in a brief article, he was able to sweep these pedestrian pedantries (some of his own along with those of his critics) into a limbo of irrelevance by showing that in a world of *scarcity and certainty* full employment would guarantee itself; that in a world of *uncertainty*, the society, by the separate choices of its individuals, must choose between concurrently consuming the equivalent of all it produces, or producing some goods whose worthwhileness depends upon an unknowable future; and that if, through the existence of *money*, the reality of this dilemma is concealed from individuals so that it appears to them possible to save and yet not to invest, the society will find itself producing only what it is willing currently to consume, while desiring to work hard enough to have incomes larger than this. This desire for work enough to make saving possible, combined with too great a doubt and perplexity to make investment bearable, is the state of under-employment. If under-employment were evenly shared it might not matter, but in fact it tends, through our institution of the firm, to mean full hours of work for some and no work at all for others.

The article we have referred to, appearing in the *Quarterly Journal of Economics* in February 1937, was called simply 'The General Theory of Employment'. Keynes here discovered, so to speak, the soul of his own work, and was able to give its expression the force of extreme brevity.

[Marshall] assumed, as Ricardo did, that the amounts of the factors of production in use were given and that the problem was to determine the way in which they would be used and their relative rewards. . . . This does not mean that they were dealing with a system in which change was ruled out, or even one in which the disappointment of expectations was ruled out. But at any given time facts and expectations were assumed to be given in a definite and calculable form; and risks, of which, though admitted, not much notice was taken, were supposed to be capable of an exact actuarial computation. The calculus of probability, though mention of it was kept in the background, was supposed to be capable of reducing uncertainty to the same calculable status as that of certainty itself.

By 'uncertain' knowledge, let me explain, I do not mean merely to distinguish what is known for certain from what is only probable. The game of roulette is not subject, in this sense, to uncertainty; . . . even the weather is only moderately uncertain. The sense in which I am using the term is that in which . . . the price of copper and the rate of interest twenty years hence [are uncertain], or the obsolescence of a new invention. . . . About these matters there is no scientific basis on which to form any calculable probability whatever. We simply do not know.

How do we manage in such circumstances to behave in a manner which saves our faces as rational, economic men? We have devised for the purpose a variety of techniques, of which much the most important are the three following:

(1) ... we largely ignore the prospect of future changes about the actual character of which we know nothing.
(2) We assume that the *existing* state of opinion as expressed in prices and the character of existing output is based on a *correct* summing up of future prospects.
(3) Knowing that our individual judgement is worthless, we endeavour to fall back on the judgement of the rest of the world which is perhaps better informed. That is, we endeavour to conform with the behaviour of the majority or the average. The psychology of a society of individuals each of whom is endeavouring to copy the others leads to what we may strictly term a *conventional* judgement.

Now a practical theory of the future based on these three principles has certain marked characteristics. In particular, being based on so flimsy a foundation, it is subject to sudden and violent changes. The practice of calmness and immobility, of certainty and security, suddenly breaks down. New fears and hopes will, without warning, take charge of human conduct. The forces of disillusion may suddenly impose a new conventional basis of valuation. All these pretty, polite techniques, made for a well-panelled Board Room and a nicely regulated market, are liable to collapse. At all times the vague panic fears and equally vague and unreasoned hopes are not really lulled, and lie but a little way below the surface.

Keynes's method: the formal analysis of equilibria and the entire repudiation of their ostensible meaning; the appeal to a herd-psychology which maintains for a time a fragile, self-hypnotizing fiction of rationality and stability, then abruptly collapses into disorder and fragmentation until 'confidence' can be restored by a mutual, universal, barely disguised 'confidence trick': seems to stem from three sources. First, his training as a mathematician and his deep impregnation with Marshall's thought imposed upon him a reliance upon static or equilibrium models. Economics, the science of response to scarcity, was centrally concerned with 'maximum' or 'minimum' problems. For such problems, formulated in the language of *continuous* functions, the differential calculus was the perfectly apt and appropriate tool, and it solved such problems with no essential reference to time. Simultaneity, in the chronological sense, was the natural setting for the problem of discovering the cheapest combination of quantities of factors to make a given output, or the combination of quantities of consumers' goods, within a given expenditure, that would maximize the consumer's satisfaction. Thus the equilibrium setting was the natural and inevitable formal frame for Keynes's reasoning, even though that reasoning was inherently concerned with the existence of ideas about the future. As to Marshall, not only his characteristic model, the suddenly disrupted equilibrium with its landslide of successive consequences, but his particular terms and his turns of phrase are found everywhere in Keynes's work. Keynes was not only Marshall's severe conscious critic but also, knowingly or not, his faithful disciple and the propagator of his ideas.

Secondly, Keynes in the *General Theory of Employment, Interest and Money* was explaining an economic earthquake, the most catastrophic depression ever known, in which, for example, in unreflated money terms, the national income of the United States was halved in three years. How could such events be described by the analysis of *equilibrium*? 'Equilibrium', said Keynes himself, 'is blither.' He meant the stable, self-regulating, automatic, optimal, full-employment-ensuring equilibrium of Ricardian and Marshallian classicism. The events of the early nineteen-thirties must be looked on, in his formal system, as the passage from one frail and precarious equilibrium to another, the tumbling, disorderly and unanalysable rush down the cliff from the plateau of 1929 to the valley floor of 1932 and 1933.

Thirdly, Keynes was closely and expertly acquainted with Stock Exchanges and other financial markets, knew their psychology at first hand, and could contrast their outward sanctimony and pretensions to knowledge with their real condition: 'the hollow and stuffed men, leaning upon each other.' No blame to them, this is the condition of humanity in its coping with the void of future time.

There is a toy called the kaleidoscope, in which three mirrors face inwards in a tall pyramid and repeat in symmetrical reflections the random mosaic of colour formed by loose pieces of stained glass on the floor of the instrument. This toy seems strangely apt as an analogue of Keynes's method.

Even the randomness of the disposition of the coloured pieces at any moment of repose suggests the *conventional* character of the economy 'at rest'. The economy is in the particular posture which prevails, because particular expectations, or rather, particular agreed formulas about the future, are for the moment widely accepted. These can change as swiftly, as completely and on as slight a provocation as the loose, ephemeral mosaic of the kaleidoscope. A twist of the hand, a piece of 'news', can shatter one picture and replace it with a different one. We must not push the comparison far, for Keynes explained each temporary pattern as a natural result of certain circumstances. These circumstances themselves, and their abrupt transitions one into another, he left unexplained. Nonetheless the kaleidoscope comparison suggests a name for Keynes's method: *kaleido-statics*.

4.2. *The Swedish model*

The contrast of method and meaning in *The General Theory of Employment, Interest and Money*, the unsuitability of the equilibrium conception to a study of the consequences of uncertainty, is more acute than it need have been. This contrast amounts to a striking paradox; for equilibrium is that model by which we are able to suppose that the participants in economic life have, at the moment of choosing their actions, a perfect knowledge of all circumstances relevant to their choices; and some part of this conception is inevitably present, whether wanted or not, in any model where things are, for however brief a time, perfectly adjusted to each other and to their general environment. To call a state of affairs an *equilibrium*, we ought at least to mean that the beliefs in the minds of all participants are mutually compatible under the test which will be applied by experience up to the end of some specified time. This time can be limited, and may if we so choose be only a day or two or an hour or two, but the conception of satisfactory, well-carpentered internal consistency and coherence in a situation, able to appear thus under the test of history for some little time at least, is part of the essential meaning of equilibrium in any model where historical time has a place. Yet Keynes found it necessary to use an equilibrium construct to discuss the consequences of ignorance and of the mutual *incompatibility* of the expectations held by this group of participants and that.

There was already in existence when Keynes was writing the *General Theory* a construction which, we may think, would have better suited his purpose. The disciples of Knut Wicksell, in particular Erik Lindahl and Gunnar Myrdal, had set themselves in the late 1920s to examine, from a wholly sympathetic viewpoint and one, indeed, of filial piety, the famous Wicksellian cumulative process in which the expectations held by business men lead them to actions which, in their outcome as a whole, falisfy those expectations in a given direction and so induce new expectations which again are self-falsified in the same direction, and so on. Wicksell's process referred to the general price level rather than to the size of general output or to the level of employment, but its essential idea, made explicit by Myrdal and Lindahl, could be applied to any kind of action and outcome. This idea consists simply in distinguishing the imaginary events and situations assigned by some individual to a still-future calendar interval, from the events and situations which appear in the record of that interval after it has passed into history. Myrdal called that conception of the contents of a segment of calendar time, which a person may entertain when he stands at the threshold of that segment, an *ex ante* view, and the numerical values composing that view *ex ante* quantities, while the account which has been recorded when the interval is past is the *ex post* view and its composing numerical values are *ex post* quantities.

Before we can use the *ex ante–ex post* construction as a vehicle for the theory of employment, we need to distinguish from each other some types of circumstance in which two things can be equal, and settle upon a notation for them. Mathematicians, it appears, seldom feel it necessary to mark such distinctions by explicit symbols, but in economics the lack of an agreed notation, or of agreed rules for choosing between the two-barred and the three-barred signs of equality which are already available, has led to confusions and fallacious argument.

4.3. *Equality by meaning, by hypothesis and by circumstances or condition*

The mode in which we shall present Keynes's theory of employment turns upon the distinction from each other of some meanings of equality. We are not here concerned with something subtle or esoteric but with plain and practical steps of thought. We shall distinguish three types of statement which assert equality of size between two measurable or calculable things. First, there can be mere dissection and rearrangement of one expression into another, mere manipulation or, in algebraic terms, expansion or simplification, or their reverse. Thus $x^2 - 2ax + a^2$ is merely another way of writing $(x - a)(x - a)$. Whatever numerical value we give to x, the numerical value of one of these expressions is the same as that of the other. A notion sufficiently close to this one to be put under the same heading is that of the equality of two things when looked at from two different points of view. When a person gives goods and receives money, and another receives the goods and gives the money, the value of what is sold is inevitably equal to the value of what is bought, because the two expressions refer to one and the same thing. Again if some entity, measurable in some respect, is defined as being in that respect the sum of other, listed, entities, we may say that the two things, the undissected and the dissected entity, are inevitably equal. Sometimes in defining a symbol, a letter of the alphabet, as standing for some more or less intricate algebraic or other expression, we are merely adopting a shorthand. In all these cases there is an evident justice in speaking of *identical* equality. All are examples of *equality by meaning*. But this latter expression covers also some further types of case.

So far we have treated that meaning which renders the two things, which have this meaning in common, equal to each other in some respect as plain, unmistakable and arising from the manifest character of the two things. Now we wish to distinguish from this situation of direct identity another situation where the identity of meaning between the two things is not apparent at a glance but is a hypothesis. So long as the hypothesis is maintained and accepted, for so long the equality also must of logical necessity be infrangible. Thus we may suppose, for the sake of some particular argument, that the weekly number of units demanded of some commodity, in some market, is one thousand minus twice the number of shillings charged per unit. This hypothesis is meant to hold true throughout the particular argument, and thus gives rise, within the argument, to an infrangible equality. Again, we may wish to express the *structure* of some nexus of variables, some system, by writing down the function, which binds these variables together, as an equation whose right-hand member is zero. Such an equation, say $F \equiv 0$, where F stands for some expression embracing several variables and supposedly able to be written out in full, or at any rate to be implicit in the nature of things, expresses a hypothetical *permanent* structure and so can be treated as an identity.

These first two types of situation giving rise to equality are, for many purposes of argument, entirely equivalent and need not be kept separate. Thus we can use for both of them one and the same symbol, borrowing for this purpose the three-barred symbol by which the algebraists indicate manipulative equality or identity, as in our example above:

$$(x - a)(x - a) \equiv x^2 - 2ax + a^2.$$

With this type of situation we can include a further one, *mandatory* equality, as when we stipulate that only those values of a function shall be considered which are all of them zero, or all of them some other constant. In such a case we might write $F(x, y, \ldots) \equiv 0$ although in a different context, or at a subsequent stage of the same argument, we recognize that $F(x, y, \ldots)$ can take non-zero values.

We shall refer hereafter to identical equality by meaning, by hypothesis and by mandate, respectively, using these expressions in the senses just explained; or alternatively to equality of types A, B and C.

In clear contrast to the foregoing types of equality, viz. equality by *identity of meaning*, by *hypothetical structure*, by *definition*, and by *stipulation*, we have the idea of *contingent* equality, equality which, even within the argument in hand, holds true only as a special, frangible, non-necessary circumstance. Economics provides the example of equality of the quantity demanded and the quantity offered, of some commodity in some market in some time-interval. This equality will come about only on condition of a particular price being established, or if equality is assumed, we can deduce the price from a knowledge of the function connecting price, as an independent variable, with quantity demanded, and the other function connecting price with quantity supplied. A particular price is the condition of demand-supply equality; demand-supply equality is a condition which pins down the price. The equality is frangible along with the frangible condition which, if and only if fulfilled, assures the equality, and the equation which expresses the equality is a *conditional* one. The two-barred sign for equality, used by mathematicians for all purposes, may conveniently be reserved by economists for expressing conditional equality.

Some of these foregoing meanings, or circumstances, of equality can be illustrated by means of a theory of employment.

4.4. *Investment and saving*

The *decision to produce* involves some definite list of a business man's possessions, some items of which list, in the course of the activity implied, for some near-future time interval, by this decision, will lose the whole or part of the economic value with which they will enter this interval, while other items will emerge from this activity with an economic value which they will owe wholly or partly to the activity of this interval. The measure of the activity implied by a decision to produce is thus a net difference of economic value; briefly, a quantity of *value added*. In reckoning this, all the items which are intended to gain or lose value through the activity of production must be brought in. Some of these items can, in a general view, be intended to be bought by the business man in the course of the interval; but nothing essential would be lost if we elected, by choosing the interval short enough, to suppose that he conceives all the items due to be transformed or to gain or lose quality by the activity, to be already in his possession at its beginning. The items whose value he proposes to create or increase by the intended activity can also be supposed to be put on the market within the interval or retained until its end.

If we suppose that no such possessions of his, intended to be physically modified during the interval, are intended to be bought or sold within the interval, the value which is expected to be added by the activity of the interval will be simply the difference between the supposed market value of the list of items at the threshold of the interval and the supposed market value of the related list of items at the end of the interval.

A number of essential questions are raised by the foregoing formulation, which we will consider before seeking to make use of it as part of the theory of employment.

What is meant here by the relatedness of the two kinds of items, those conceived to be in the business man's possession at the threshold and those at the close of the interval? The final list must derive none of its value from initial items not included in the initial list, and the initial list must contribute value only to items included in the final list. To achieve this, the initial list must comprehend the whole, or a self-contained part, of the business man's operations. He may be the owner of several firms, each with its own means of production and types of product, but a single decision to produce must relate to only one firm.

Since at the moment of a business man's decision to produce in a named calendar interval, this interval necessarily lies wholly in his future, the value which specific productive activity will add to a given list of initial possessions is conjectural. We are bound to suppose that in making his decision to produce, the business man has in mind a number of rival hypotheses, all of which he accepts as in some degree possible, about the quantity of value which will thus be added. Nevertheless we shall here suppose him to elect a single quantity to represent this range of possibilities. We may, for example, take this representative quantity to be the one he would elect if compelled to bet a moderate amount on one quantity only. Since in fact, in his decision to produce, he may be staking a sum which is considerable, rather than moderate, in relation to the total value of his owned resources (his fortune), he may choose the character in detail, and the scale, of his proposed production, so as to guard against the worst consequences of a wrong conjecture about the value which will be added. But once he has made, in a detailed formula, the decision to produce, whether this decision be of a bold or cautious kind, we shall suppose the business man to elect only a single number as his hypothesis concerning the value which his intended productive operation of the interval will add to his possessions as a whole.

Like the equilibrium model, the different model, which we are here seeking to cast with Keynesian substance in a Stockholm mould as an explanation of the possibility of general unemployment, draws its essential character from its assumptions about the basis of knowledge and the sources of ideas available to the members of the society, and about the uses that they make of them. In direct contrast to the equilibrium model, the employment model supposes that each person's and especially each business man's basis of relevant knowledge, so far from being perfect, is glaringly insufficient, and that thus the way is open for the entry into his mind of hopes and fears prompted by the slightest events. His awareness of this inadequacy of his dossier of knowledge is what we mean by uncertainty, and uncertainty is inseparable from the Keynesian account of unemployment. There are, however, many very diverse schemes by which the detached observer, whose standpoint we are occupying, can incorporate into his theories a recognition of the participant's uncertainty. We have elected that method which simplifies the 'Stockholm' part of our presentation, and which is indeed, despite recent refinements of the Stockholm school's work, almost essential to it, namely, the supposition that the business man represents his range of hypotheses, about the quantity of value added that he will achieve, by a *single* hypothesis.

Whatever the business man may actually expect concerning the course of prices between the beginning and the end of the productive interval, and whatever effect these expectations may have on his decision as to what and how much to produce, consistency in measuring quantities of value added requires this measurement to be made at prices which are in some sense constant. The list of relevant possessions with which he expects to enter the interval, and the list with which he expects to emerge from it, are different. Thus we cannot simply stipulate that each item shall be valued at the same prices in each situation. We are faced with one of the inescapable imprecisions of economic theory, the index number problem. The only stipulation we can make, in order to ensure that the value added measures the technical or physical activity of production and not merely a change of price of technically unchanged items, is that the initial and final lists of possessions shall be considered to be valued either at unchanged prices, where similar items appear in both lists, or at prices deflated by a suitable index in other cases. However, since the productive interval is for other reasons to be taken as short, and as lying in the business man's near or immediate future, price changes can perhaps be ignored.

We have now given a meaning to the expression *value of a production decision* of an individual business man. By it we mean the value which, according to his representative hypothesis, will be added to the value of some given list of his possessions during that calendar interval to which his production decision refers. This idea is, as it were, the elementary particle of the theory of employment. By its means we seek to give a description of what is implied, for the immediate economic future of the society we are studying, by the internal decision-structure of a given moment. For this purpose we have, first, to define very briefly the institutional framework of the supposed society, in especial as to the economic role of its government; secondly to say whether or not it is economically isolated and self-contained; thirdly to aggregate the values of the production decisions taken at some one moment, by all those in the society (namely, its business men in the widest sense, and perhaps its government) empowered to take them, and to stipulate that these decisions shall all refer to one and the same calendar interval and that no production decisions, taken at other moments, shall refer to this interval; fourthly, to consider what action by the business man is entailed by his decision to produce; fifthly, to make assumptions about the expectations and intentions of those who will enjoy the fruits of the intended production of the interval, concerning their disposal of these fruits; and lastly, to study the *interplay* of the actions of this kind and that decided upon by the business men and those they employ, and thus to see what outcome, at the end of the interval we are considering, is implied for the society as a whole by the various independent decisions of its members and classes of members.

If at first we suppose that the society has no government and no relations with anything outside itself, and if by *business men* we understand all those who, being in command of lists of suitable possessions, can take effective decisions to produce, then all production in the society will flow from production decisions of business men. In order to be able to treat the list of all those production decisions which refer to a given calendar interval, as guaranteeing that the technical activities specified in these decisions will be carried out, we have, first, to elect to mean by decision a psychic commitment from which the decision-maker will not withdraw except through a physical impossibility of executing it; and such a meaning for decision will be the more reasonable if we identify the moment of decision with the threshold of the production interval and if we make that interval 'short'; secondly, we have to suppose that the decision-maker has knowledge enough of the list of possessions with which he will enter the interval, to be able to make his decision correspond, in this respect, with his circumstances; and lastly, we have to suppose that the hired services of other people or other people's possessions, which the business men will require in order to execute their production decisions, will be available to all of them at once in sufficient quantities to fulfil the whole list of all their respective production decisions at prices which will induce them to make those decisions.

The first two of these requirements call for no discussion: we are free to design our model on these lines if we like. The third, however, calls for some mechanism or facilities for adjusting to each other, on one hand the quantities of productive services which people other than business men as such will supply to the business men at this set or that of prices or rates of hire, and on the other hand the quantities which the business men deem it worth while to hire at these prices. In other words, we have again an epistemic problem: each business man, in order to decide how much to produce, with his given threshold possessions, during the interval, needs to know what expense he will incur, by this or that scale of production. additional to the sacrifice of value of some of his threshold possessions. Or in yet other words again, for each rival productive operation open to him, how much must he subtract from its expected value added, to find what it will contribute, according to his representative expectation, to his own wealth? For we shall suppose each production decision to be that which appears to the business man concerned to promise him the largest available profit.

This epistemic condition can be met by supposing that what we shall call hired services, that is, all the means of production called for by a given production decision, other than those means comprised in the business man's threshold possessions, will be secured by contracts signed at the threshold of the interval. These contracts will specify the payments to be made to the suppliers of hired services and thus will enable both the business man and his suppliers of hired services to know their *expected income of the interval*. The suppliers of hired services can read off their contractual incomes from the contracts they have been induced to sign. The business man has merely to subtract the total of these payments, which he has contracted to make, from the value, according to his representative expectation, of his production decision. With these assumptions, the values of all the production decisions taken at a given moment, which by assumption all refer to the immediately future interval of specified length and are the only ones referring to it, and which account for the whole production intended to take place in this interval, can be legitimately added together to give an *aggregate value of intended production of the interval*, viz. E_A; by our institutional assumptions, this E_A includes every value-item which is intended to be genuinely created in the interval, and it excludes everything else. It is therefore what we mean by the society's aggregate of expected incomes, Y_A. Thus we can write

$$Y_A \equiv E_A, \tag{1}$$

here using the three-barred symbol to mean identical equality of type A, and showing, by this equation (1), the meaning or source of *income*.

It is of little immediate importance to us that the business men's grounds for expecting a specific absolute share of this aggregate are quite different from those of the suppliers of hired services for expecting theirs. For the latter, this basis is a contract, only imperilled by the possibility that the business men may be unable to honour it even out of reserves, which, if the interval is short, is a very remote possibility. In their capacity as disposers of expected income, we can treat all the members of the society as giving to 'expected income' one and the same meaning. We are seeking to describe the decision-structure of that particular moment when the business men take their decisions to produce. There is a second set of decisions which we can quite naturally suppose to be taken at that same moment, for this is the moment when income-expectations also are formed. Each member of the society must decide what part of his expected income he will spend on consumption and what part he will leave unspent, that is, will save. These two parts evidently exhaust the aggregate of expected incomes and we can write

$$Y_A \equiv C_A + S_A, \tag{2}$$

where C_A stands for aggregate consumption intentions and S_A stands for the aggregate of income residuals after consumption intentions are provided for. Equation (2) expresses an identical equality of type A. Since the left-hand sides of (1) and (2) are also identical in sense A, a third identity of the same type will read

$$E_A \equiv C_A + S_A. \tag{3}$$

It is sometimes thought, and declared, that an identity can tell us nothing. Yet this identity directly raises the crucial question of employment theory. If S_A is greater than zero; if, that is, C_A is less than E_A; to whom can those products be sold, which cannot be sold to consumers as such? In what market can the business men expect to realize in cash that part of the value of their production decisions, which is not matched by the consumption decisions of the income disposers all taken together?

The decision-moment of our model involves two more classes of decisions besides those of how much to produce and of how much to spend on consumption. The business man must decide how much, at the end of the interval, he will sell and also how much, at the end of the interval, he will buy from other business men for the purpose of production in further intervals beyond the immediate one. All these quantities, since each may involve physically heterogeneous goods, must of course be conceived and expressed to himself by the business man in terms of value at given or comparable prices. These decisions, taken at the threshold of the interval, prescribe action to be taken at its end, for we have elected to simplify the meaning and measure of production by supposing that no buying and selling occur in the interior of the interval. Suppose now that a business man decides he will sell, at the end of the interval, goods of a value s, and that s is greater than his intended value-added v. Such a relation of the two quantities will be natural, for the productive operation consists in diminishing the value of the particular items which make up his initial list (these items being 'materials' and 'tools') and more than replacing the lost value by that of newly constituted items ('products') which are designed for sale. Let us now represent by i the value of goods which his third type of decision, made, of course, along with his other decisions, at the threshold of the interval, prescribes that he shall buy from other business men at the end of the interval, and let us consider the implication of various conceivable relations between i and the difference $s - v$.

Our search is for a source of demand, additional to that of consumers as such, for the results of intended *production*, that is, for goods representing *value added*. But the intended purchases, i, of a business man as such are only a demand for value added in so far as they are not *offset by his intended sales in excess* of his value added. Each business man as such, by his intended business purchases, makes a net contribution to the society's aggregate of intended demands for its value added, and this contribution, $i_n \equiv i - (s - v)$, may be positive or negative. Value added must by its meaning be reckoned *after* allowance for the loss of value suffered, in the act of production, by the business man's initial list of possessions. All that part of i which merely serves to make good this loss can make no contribution to the demand for value added.

Let us express the situation in more conventional terms. $s - v$ is the *depreciation* which the business man's equipment of tools and materials, with which he is entering upon the interval, will suffer because of his intended production in the interval. Only if his intended gross investment i exceeds numerically the expected depreciation $s - v$ will it make any contribution towards providing a demand equivalent to some part of his intended value added. When we are asking what quantity of demand for the society's aggregate of intended value added will be provided by investment decisions, it is evidently appropriate to take the algebraic sum of the quantities, one for each business man, $i_n \equiv i - (s - v)$. This aggregate $I_n \equiv \Sigma i_n$, is the society's *aggregate intended net investment.* In the composition of this aggregate there is no multiple counting, for each business man's contribution to it is reckoned after allowing for those of his purchases of materials and tools which merely offset his excess of goods sold over goods produced. It is accordingly this aggregate which we may legitimately add to the aggregate of intended consumption spending, C, to get the society's whole intended demand for value added. This aggregate intended effective demand D is

$$D \equiv C_A + I_n, \tag{4}$$

where the identity sign, as in the two preceding definitional equations, indicates identical equality of type A.

The four numbered equations which this chapter has so far displayed are all of them identities. (1) is definitional; (2) and (3) we may say, are dissectional, showing how some quantity can be looked on as the sum of others which, for some reason, are separately interesting or each capable of being separately and usefully accounted for. Equation (4) can be looked on either as a definition or as a dissection of aggregate effective demand. The purpose of our whole argument, however, is to state a *condition* on whose fulfilment the self-consistency, the coherence, of the decision-structure, the latent mutual justification of its composing decisions, depends. This necessary condition is that aggregate effective demand shall equal the aggregate of intended value added, $D = E_A$, and since these two symbols are the respective left-hand members of equations (3) and (4), their equality implies the equality also of the right-hand members of those equations:

$$C_A + S_A = C_A + I_n$$

or

$$S_A = I_n. \tag{5}$$

The famous equality of saving and investment, on which Keynes so much insisted, turns out to have two entirely distinct meanings. For let us place ourselves at the end of some interval, and using for all valuations the prices just then established by the market, let us write E_p for the society's aggregate value added of this past interval, according to a record, conceivable in principle because the contents of the interval can now be seen *ex post* as things which happened in fact, which gives a consistent account of those contents agreed by everybody. The society's aggregate income of the interval, as shown in the record *ex post*, will be simply the aggregate value added and we can say

$$Y_p \equiv E_p. \qquad (6)$$

The society's aggregate spending on consumption, which occurs at our moment of observation, can also be treated as an observable fact C_p. When this spending is compared with E_p there will be a difference I_p representing the net augmentation, measured in value, which has been brought to the society's aggregate list of possessions by the events of the just-past interval, namely the production of goods worth E_p and the withdrawal for consumption of goods worth C_p. This net augmentation is the *net investment ex post* of the interval. But since $Y_p \equiv E_p$ by definition, the difference $E_p - C_p \equiv Y_p - C_p$, where again the sign of identical equality indicates equality by meaning. But the difference $Y_p - C_p$ is the *unspent income*, that is to say, the *saving*, of the just-past interval, and so, using again the sign of identical equality by meaning, we have

$$I_p \equiv S_p. \qquad (7)$$

When, from the end of an interval, we look at the agreed record of its events, net investment *ex post* and saving *ex post* are identically equal by meaning. But when, as in the foregoing pages, we look from the threshold, *ex ante*, we can see that the equality of saving with net investment is in absolute contrast with identity: it is a frangible *condition* which may or may not be fulfilled. Keynes would have saved himself great difficulty in exposition, and some of his expositors endless confusions of thought, if the *ex ante–ex post* formula and mode of thought had come to his notice before he wrote the *General Theory*.

4.5. *The Multiplier: process and equilibrium*

Suppose, then, that the condition $I_A = S_A$ is not satisfied. When the business men's present moment and temporal viewpoint has reached the end of the interval, the quantity of money then offered them for goods will be greater or less than the supposition on which their production decisions had been based. The business men, all taken together, can sell more goods, or sell goods more profitably, than they had expected, or vice versa. If therefore we assume that this divergence of fact from earlier expectation is the only relevant news which they receive, it will be reasonable to say that their production decisions for the new interval, at whose threshold they have arrived, will be different in aggregate value from those they took for the former interval. But without further detailed and precise assumptions this is as far as we can go. Our condition, $I_A = S_A$, gives us a choice of two paths. We can be content to say that provided this condition is satisfied, the aggregate value (at constant prices) of production decisions will continue from threshold to threshold of successive intervals to be the same, in the absence of strong disturbances from invention or technical innovation, from fashion, from politics or from natural convulsions such as seasons of famine or glut over large areas. If from such sources an equilibrium, $I_A = S_A$, is disturbed, we shall, if we adopt this first path, resign ourselves to say nothing beyond the direction of change, an increase or decrease of E, aggregate production per unit interval, that is, of *output*. For this path is an expression of that basic methodological attitude which insists that only equilibrium, in one or another sense, is an orderly and structured conception or state of affairs such as can be analysed and made sense of. The tumbling progress from one equilibrium to another is essentially marked by the fog-bound uncertainty, mis-information and mistrust of the participants, and their responses to the scarcely interpretable scraps of guidance available to them are necessarily non-rational and therefore unpredictable. This view is what we have sought to suggest by the name *kaleido-statics*.

Let us use the word *engine* to mean, as it does in its physical sense, a structure of precise design and dimensions, whose movements, that is, the succession of states it will be in at a succession of dates, if started off from a given state with a push of given strength, are determined by that structure. The second path, by which we can follow out the consequences of non-fulfilment of $I_A = S_A$, is to construct an economic engine which, when sufficiently precise assumptions are built into it, will describe for us the whole process of movement from one equilibrium to another, showing a series of states of affairs, or (equivalently) of transitions from one state to another, which together compose a pattern *entailed* by the design of the engine together with its initial state and the character of the initial disturbance. It sounds as though an engine of this kind will give us a much more full and satisfying answer to the question: What happens when equilibrium, $I_A = S_A$, is replaced by some other state of affairs? However, we shall not get this more explicit answer for nothing. To claim that when one equilibrium is broken, there will be a passage, occupying some unspecified time, to a new one, and that this new one will, according to the circumstances of the disruption of the earlier equilibrium, involve a higher or lower aggregate income of the society, requires far less in the way of arbitrarily chosen detailed and precise assumptions than the construction of an engine that will fill in the whole course of events. We can, of course, construct many or infinitely many such engines, and indeed each value in the range of values assignable to each of the parameters in the algebraic expression of such an engine will represent a different specific model. The smallest change in a parameter can sometimes alter the behaviour of the model from stability to explosion. But this very multiplicity of possible paths, which the course of events can follow, leaves us in an ignorance scarcely diminished by the possession of these models, except for the slender hope, in any concrete situation, that statistics will provide reliable and precise numerical values for the parameters, and that the models themselves, being necessarily kept simple enough for analysis, will not prove to have grossly over-simplified reality.

What we have called an engine is of course the creation and instrument of an outside observer, one who can simultaneously treat as objective and known fact the situations or events of many different dates. He can thus consider a stretch of time, divide it into unit intervals, and make assumptions which bind together into an indivisible structure the contents of the different intervals or of the moments which separate them. The conception called the Multiplier illustrates our concept of an engine in a very simple and dissectible form which has also a great practical relevance. In his famous article of 1931 Professor Richard Kahn showed that an increment ΔI_A of the society's intended net investment will, on very plausible and simple assumptions, lead to an increment ΔY_A of the society's expected income such that ΔY_A will be greater than ΔI_A in a ratio, called the Multiplier, numerically depending on what proportion, out of any promised increment of income, the society allots to intended extra consumption. This proposition became part of the core of the *General Theory of Employment, Interest and Money*, but its mechanism was variously conceived and interpreted even by Keynes himself:*

I have found, however, . . . some confusion between the logical theory of the multiplier, which holds good continuously, without time-lag, at all moments of time, and the consequences of an expansion in the capital-goods industries which take gradual effect, subject to time-lag and only after an interval.

The 'logical theory' which 'holds good continuously, without time-lag, at all moments of time' is not that of the Multiplier but that of the *marginal propensity to consume*, the ratio $\Delta C_A / \Delta Y_A$ of the society's extra intended consumption to its extra promised income. This propensity expresses the tastes, habits, outlook and in general the character or *psyche* of the members of the society, modified perhaps by their conception of their immediate circumstances and prospects. It may plainly be said to operate at all times. But the Multiplier is a calculation of the response of different groups of people to each other's actions, as those actions are performed and become known, and Keynes has only two proposals as to how this chain of events can be looked on as instantaneous. One is to assume (*General Theory*, p. 122) that the 'change in aggregate investment has been foreseen sufficiently in advance for the consumption industries to advance *pari passu* with the capital-goods industries . . .'. Such foresight might, broadly, be achieved by such an instru-

* *General Theory*, p. 122.

ment of co-ordination as the French *Commissariat du Plan* or the British *National Economic Development Council*, but it was not a relevant contemporary assumption for Keynes. Keynes's other approach, which lurks in the background of his argument, is a wholly fallacious resort to the irrelevant *ex post* identity of saving and net investment. Since saving and investment are necessarily equal, he seems to be saying, the ratio of extra income to extra net investment will at all times be equal to that of extra income to extra saving, and the latter ratio is a 'propensity' always at work with a quantitative effect which we broadly know. What has gone wrong? At bottom it is the neglect of two intimately linked distinctions: that between *ex ante* and *ex post* quantifications, and that between conditional and identical equality. The net investment which actively presses on the course of events is the *imagined, desired, intended* net investment of business men, something which they decide to attempt; the net investment which, *ex post*, is identically equal to saving is the passive balancing residual of production and consumption. Aggregate intended net investment can *become* equal to aggregate intended saving. There may be psychic pressures and institutional mechanisms (the market, or the 'Plan') which make the gap between these magnitudes successively smaller as we look at successive dates. But their equality is a *condition* which, at any one date, may be fulfilled or unfulfilled. By contrast, the *ex post identical* equality of saving and net investment is logically incapable of being *attained*, it cannot be a goal, a tendency, a test, a stage of evolution, a position of repose, a *special*, as distinct from an eternal and invariable, state of things, we cannot move towards it or away from it, we cannot break it or restore it or be attracted or repelled by it or observe it or explain it, it *is* (by our own choice of categories and meanings for words).

Since identities cannot explain a process nor state a condition towards the fulfilment of which psychic forces will drive the society, we must not be content merely to manipulate the marginal propensity to consume until it looks like the Multiplier. But if we think that any description of a process of adjustment will inevitably be arbitrary and artificial, and are content to claim that the society will somehow force its way to a new equilibrium when its former one has been destroyed, we can quite legitimately compare these two equilibrium situations and form the ratio of the difference of their respective aggregates of income to the difference of their respective aggregates of net investment. Since in calling these situations equilibria we mean that in each of them there is an *ex ante* equality of aggregate saving and aggregate net investment, the ratio $\Delta Y_A/\Delta I_A$ will be equal to the ratio $\Delta Y_A/\Delta S_A$, and it follows that if we have any means of calculating the latter its numerical value will serve as that of the former.

Let us label quantities belonging to the first of the two equilibria by the subscript 1, as Y_1 for its aggregate income, S_1 for its aggregate saving, C_1 for its aggregate consumption spending; and let us similarly write Y_2, S_2 and C_2 for the aggregate income, saving, and consumption of the second equilibrium. Then by the meanings we have given to the words income, saving and consumption, we have

$$S_2 \equiv Y_2 - C_2,$$

$$S_1 \equiv Y_1 - C_1$$

and $$S_2 - S_1 \equiv Y_2 - Y_1 - (C_2 - C_1),$$

which we can write $$\Delta S \equiv \Delta Y - \Delta C, \tag{8}$$

using the sign Δ to mean 'take the difference between two numerical values' of some variable. Equation (8) is the same as

$$\Delta S \equiv \Delta Y - \Delta Y \frac{\Delta C}{\Delta Y},$$

that is, $$\Delta S \equiv \Delta Y \left(1 - \frac{\Delta C}{\Delta Y}\right).$$

Dividing both sides by ΔS and by $\left(1 - \frac{\Delta C}{\Delta Y}\right)$ we have finally

$$\frac{1}{1 - \frac{\Delta C}{\Delta Y}} \equiv \frac{\Delta Y}{\Delta S}. \tag{9}$$

All we have done is to manipulate identities, and all we have got is an identity. This identity states the manipulative relation between the two expressions:

$\frac{\Delta Y}{\Delta S}$ the ratio of extra income to extra saving

when the word 'extra' is understood to mean that these 'extra' quantities are associated with and correspond to each other; and

$\frac{\Delta C}{\Delta Y}$ the ratio of extra consumption spending to extra income

when, again, we mean that these extra quantities go together, and both arise from the comparison of the same two equilibria. Now $\frac{\Delta Y}{\Delta S}$ is numerically equal, *when we are comparing equilibria*, to the Multiplier ratio of intended net investment to expected income, $\frac{\Delta Y_A}{\Delta I_A}$; and $\frac{\Delta C}{\Delta Y}$ measures the society's marginal propensity to consume. Thus our equation (9), applied to the comparison of *two equilibrium situations*, gives us the numerical value of the Multiplier in terms of one of the society's own characteristics, its marginal propensity to consume. How can we sum up this result? We can write the conditional equation

$$\frac{\Delta Y_A}{\Delta I_A} = \frac{1}{1 - \frac{\Delta C_A}{\Delta Y_A}} \qquad (10)$$

valid only for the comparison of two equilibria.

From this equation a train of important consequences, long since familiar, can be deduced. The larger the society's marginal propensity to consume, the larger will be the multiplier. Thus if we now assume that our society has a government, any measure adopted by this government, such as a redistribution of income amongst individuals, which alters the society's marginal propensity to consume, can have an effect on the level of maintainable production and employment. The government can seek by fiscal or monetary means to influence the aggregate intended investment of business men, or can itself add to that aggregate some intended investment of its own, and in each of these ways can alter the 'multiplicand' and thus with a *given* Multiplier alter the level of maintainable production and employment. These ideas are not part of our present concern, and we wish instead to follow the 'second path', referred to above, in studying the outcome of inequality between intended net investment and intended saving.

Let us again suppose that our society has no government, so that all economic actions are those of individuals in one or other of their two capacities, as income disposers or as business men. Being outside observers we can give simultaneous place in our thoughts to all the instants and intervals of a stretch of time. We can look upon the situations and events of this stretch of time as the manifestation of the inherent design or structure of an economic 'engine'. For this purpose we divide the stretch of time into equal intervals called *income periods*. At the threshold of each such period, the business men decide upon their production to be done within the period and upon their sales and investment to be done at its end; and also at the threshold, each member of the society, in his capacity as income-disposer, having in mind his expected income for the period, decides in what proportions, at the end of the period, he will divide it between spending on consumption and non-spending, that is, saving.

Aggregative or 'macro-economic' analysis is necessarily imprecise. It is not the society as a whole which decides upon the proportion of its aggregate of expected incomes that it will spend on consumption, but each individual member of the society who decides what proportion of his own expected income he will so spend. The influence of each such individual decision upon the aggregative proportion depends, of course, on the size of the individual income in question. The marginal propensity to consume of the society as a whole is a weighted average of the individual members' propensities, the weights being the sizes of the individual expected incomes. It follows that a given aggregate income, differently composed of individual incomes of this size and that, will in general be differently divided between intended consumption spending and intended saving. This will be so without there needing to be any change in the personal propensity to consume of any individual. Now as we scan the series of income periods from earlier to later, we shall see some individuals, each with his own marginal propensity to consume, gaining or losing income faster than other individuals with a different set of personal propensities. The weighting of the average will change. For the model or 'engine' we now wish to construct, we nevertheless wish to assume for the society as a whole an aggregative marginal propensity to consume which is constant from period to period. Many different suppositions would serve this purpose. We can assume a close uniformity of individual propensities, or a very small change in proportionate distribution of income and therefore in weighting, or some cancellation of one kind of change by the other: no matter which, so long as it enables us to speak of the society's marginal propensity to consume as a constant. We will write this constant k.

The only further assumption we need is that, at each threshold, business men increase their aggregate value of intended production by exactly the excess of the demand they are actually experiencing at this threshold over their production of the just-elapsed period. Some assumption about the relation of intended production of the new period to experienced relation of demand and production in the old period is an indispensable link in the mechanism, yet few writers on the Multiplier supply one. Any such assumption is special and arbitrary. The one we have made is the simplest possible, and is indeed implicit in all those explanations which treat the Multiplier as a process. At the threshold of each period, then, those decisions to buy goods for consumption or for investment are actually executed, which were taken one period earlier, at the threshold of the just-elapsed period. If, at threshold n, the aggregate of expected incomes is greater by ΔY_n than it was at threshold $n - 1$, the consumption-demand actually exercised at threshold $n + 1$ will exceed that actually exercised at threshold n by k times ΔY_n, where $0 < k < 1$. The 'Multiplier process' which results from these assumptions can be displayed in a table (see Table 4.1): Here we have supposed that, in comparison with a base period 0, intended net investment is increased at the threshold of period 1 by one unit (of any size we choose) and maintained at this new higher level through all subsequent periods. At the threshold of period 2, therefore, production decisions in the aggregate are increased, as compared with those of the threshold of period 0, by whatever value constitutes our unit of net investment. This can be anything we choose, for example, £1 million, but by calling it one unit, and representing it by a 1 in each place in the top row of our table, we simplify the look of our algebra. Net investment is an augmentation, of some or all business men's list of productive possessions, which occurs at some date, preceded and followed at other dates by similar increases or

TABLE 4.1

Threshold of period	1	2	3	4	5
Increment, compared with period 0, of aggregate					
Intended net investment	1	1	1	1	
Expected income		1	$1+k$	$1+k+k^2$	$1+k+k^2+k^3$
Intended consumption spending		k	$k+k^2$	$k+k^2+k^3$	$k+k^2+k^3+k^4$

declines. Thus net investment is measured by value *per unit of time*, and in writing a row of 1's along the top of our table, we indicate that an extra and (as we can assert, from our vantage point of detached observer) a permanent flow of net investment has been added to the aggregate production flow of the society and thus to the aggregate of expected incomes of the society. The same unit of quantification, say of £1 million per period, will serve of course for the expression of aggregate income and of aggregate consumption-spending. At the threshold of period 2 no other addition, except this unit extra flow of net investment, is added to the aggregate of expected incomes, as compared with period 0, for the extra consumption-spending, which the sudden emergence of these new expectations of income induce, will be executed, and responded to by business men in their production decisions, only at the threshold of period 3. At the threshold of period 3, aggregate production decisions and hence aggregate expected incomes will be higher than those at the threshold of period 0 by two distinct increments: first the extra production induced by (and equal to) the unit incremental investment flow, and secondly by the increment, which now occurs, of production decisions as a response to increased consumption-spending. The increase in consumption spending will be k times the increase which occurred one period earlier in aggregate expected income, which increase itself was of one unit. Accordingly at the threshold of period 3, the value of production decisions exceeds the level it had at the threshold of period 0 by $1 + k$. At this same threshold, aggregate intended consumption-spending exceeds the level it had in period 0 by $k + k^2$. At threshold 4, production decisions exceed those of period 0 by 1 (increment of investment) + $(k + k^2)$, the contents of the bracket being the extra production (as compared with period 0) induced by the extra consumption-spending. How many periods will have to elapse before, with our supposedly constant marginal propensity to consume of k greater than zero and less than unity, the ratio of extra expected income to extra intended net investment will have reached a stable value? In principle, infinitely many. For let us label the extra expected income and the extra intended net investment of each threshold, compared with those of period 0, by writing the number of the threshold as a subscript, thus:

$\Delta Y_{A,1}$ the excess of expected aggregate income at threshold 1 over that at threshold 0,

$\Delta Y_{A,2}$ the excess of expected aggregate income at threshold 2 over that at threshold 0,

....

$\Delta Y_{A,j}$ the excess of expected aggregate income at threshold j over that at threshold 0,

and similarly $\Delta I_{A,j}$ for the excess of intended net investment at each threshold j over that of threshold 0. $\Delta I_{A,j} = 1$, according to our suppositions, for all (possible natural numbers represented by) j. At any threshold j, the Multiplier ratio for that threshold will be

$$\Delta Y_{A,j}/\Delta I_{A,j} = (1 + k + k^2 + \ldots + k^{j-2})/1$$
$$= 1 + k + k^2 + \ldots + k^{j-2}.$$

By a trivial manipulation,* we can show that this series sums to $\frac{1 - k^{j-1}}{1 - k}$. Now since $0 < k < 1$ it follows that k^{j-1} gets smaller as $j - 1$ gets bigger, and as our glance travels to successive thresholds we see the numerical value of the Multiplier increasing by these diminishing amounts. If we suppose j to increase beyond all bounds or 'tend to infinity', k^j will tend to zero, and so the Multiplier ratio approaches asymptotically the limit value $\frac{1}{1 - k}$, the value we found by comparing a supposedly *attained* new equilibrium position with the old:

$$\Delta Y_{A,j}/\Delta I_{A,j} \equiv \sum_{x=0}^{j-1} k^x \rightarrow \frac{1}{1-k} \quad \text{as} \quad j \rightarrow \infty.$$

All the entries of Table 4.1 are quantifications *ex ante*, yet this table is meant to show the structure and working of the Multiplier 'engine'. At the moment when a numerical value is assigned *ex ante* by a participant, there can of course be no dependence of anything on, or determination of anything by, the semantically and numerically distinct quantity which, at a different and later 'present moment', will take the place of this *ex ante* quantity. Thus a table which consists of so-called *ex ante* quantities, some belonging to later dates than others, can only exist or have meaning in the thought of the outside and extra-temporal observer, not in that of a participant. But we must go further in interpreting it than this. For the structure and working of the 'engine' consist precisely in such a dependence of *ex ante* quantities on *ex post* quantities, and so the table must be understood to conceal within its meaning the *ex post* quantities which will be the consequence of the execution of the intentions and decisions which it explicitly displays. We have in fact adopted a rule for the emergence of *ex post* from *ex ante* quantities, namely the assumption that intentions and

* We multiply the series $S = 1 + k + k^2 + \ldots + k^{j-2}$

by k to get $kS = k + k^2 + \ldots + k^{j-2} + k^{j-1}$

so that $S - kS = S(1 - k) = 1 - k^{j-1}$

and $S = \frac{1 - k^{j-1}}{1 - k}$.

decisions to produce and to lay out money are commitments which will be executed if this is logically possible. Lack of possibility would arise, within our own concerns and thus within the model itself, through a clash of such intentions. Let us ask, then, whether, within this model, business men's intentions to perform investment can be always realized? Their intentions, adopted at, say, threshold j to purchase productive possessions from each other at threshold $j+1$ can, we assume, always be carried out. But these intentions are interpreted by them at threshold j as comprising so-and-so much making good of depletion, so-and-so much net investment. If demand at threshold $j+1$ proves larger than they had assumed, depletion will be greater and net investment less than they had supposed. This is how the course of realized, *ex post* events, implied by our assumptions and latent in Table 4.1, must be understood.

By examining a few particular thresholds, which however we must now think of rather as the terminal dates of already elapsed periods than as the beginnings of 'future' ones, we can see how $I_{P,j}$, the realized, recorded net investment of the period ending at date j, behaves when looked on as a function of j. Using the subscript P to indicate *ex post* quantities we have first of all

$E_{P,j}$ the aggregate of realized production, i.e. value added in all firms taken together, in the period ending at j,

$Y_{P,j}$ the aggregate of realized incomes of the period ending at j.

There is now an important question which we can no longer avoid. The structure and working of our engine assume that realized sales of goods will often be larger in physical quantity, and therefore in value at the *ex ante* assumed prices, than was expected or assumed when the production decisions were taken. Are we to suppose that the prices at which realized production of an elapsed period is reckoned are unaffected by this? We shall suppose so, for there is nothing in our model to make this a strained or artificial assumption. The purpose of the 'constant price' accounting which we adopted in describing the sets of *ex ante* decisions, intentions and suppositions is to make possible the comparison of consistently measured 'real' quantities of composite 'general output'. The same purpose requires to be served in comparing realized with expected results of any period, and the use of unchanged prices is from this point of view and for this purpose, indispensable. Now we have assumed that decisions to produce can and will be executed, and also that decisions to spend on consumption, or on productive goods, can and will be executed. Such assumptions may well seem to be opposed to the spirit of an *ex ante* analysis, since so far as production, consumption and gross investment are concerned, they abolish the distinction between *ex ante* and *ex post*. This fact serves to emphasize the artificial nature of an 'engine' such as we are describing. For some such assumptions are unavoidable in its construction, and yet are only possible at all because we have arrogated to ourselves the stance of an 'outside observer'. The basic difficulty and danger, in constructing a theoretical 'engine', is how to set, to make explicit, and to *observe*, limits to the implied knowledge and power of such an outside observer. One of our purposes in spelling out the working of our model is to throw such difficulties into sharp relief.

By our assumptions, then,

$$E_{P,j} \equiv E_{A,j-1} \tag{11}$$

and we may conveniently remind ourselves here that

$$Y_{A,j} \equiv E_{A,j}.$$

Further,

$$C_{P,j} \equiv C_{A,j-1}. \tag{12}$$

The meaning we assign to *realized net investment of the period* ending at j is

$$I_{P,j} \equiv E_{P,j} - C_{P,j}$$

which, by equations (11) and (12) above, gives

$$I_{P,j} \equiv Y_{A,j-1} - C_{A,j-1}.$$

This equality is true in general, i.e. of all periods including period 0, and so by subtraction we have

$$\Delta I_{P,j} \equiv \Delta Y_{A,j-1} - \Delta C_{A,j-1}.$$

At dates 3, 4, 5 we thus have

$$\Delta I_{P,3} = 1 - k,$$

$$\Delta I_{P,4} = 1 + k - (k + k^2) = 1 - k^2,$$

$$\Delta I_{P,5} = 1 + k + k^2 - (k + k^2 + k^3) = 1 - k^3,$$

and in general evidently

$$\Delta I_{P,j} \equiv 1 - k^{(j-2)}. \tag{13}$$

From equation (13) it is plain that as we scan the periods in succession, we see the increment, by which *ex post* net investment of the period ending at j exceeds that of period 0, rising steadily towards the (constant) level of *intended* net investment. For the latter is 1, and *ex post* net investment falls short of this by the subtrahend $k^{(j-2)}$ which is a decreasing function of j.

The income and investment composing the Multiplier ratio as we have interpreted it are *ex ante* quantities. Only thus can the Multiplier offer an explanation of how events arise from human decisions based, themselves, upon expectations. But if we wish we can define an *ex post* Multiplier, viz.

$$Y_{P,j}/I_{P,j} \equiv (1 + k + \ldots + k^{(j-3)})/(1 - k^{(j-2)})$$

$$\equiv \frac{1}{1-k},$$

a result which can be verified by multiplying both forms of the expression by $1 - k$ and thus making both expressions equal to unity. It thus appears that the *ex post* Multiplier is a constant independent of j. We thus tie up a loose end in our study of the Multiplier. For under the *ex ante* view we had a Multiplier ratio increasing with j and a *multiplicand*, viz. $\Delta I_{A,j} = 1$, which remained constant. Under the *ex post* view we found that the multiplicand increases with j but the Multiplier ratio is constant. Our main purpose in this section of Chapter 4 has been to examine the meaning of an 'engine', of which the Multiplier process provides a very simple illustration, and to show that such an engine, when built of *ex ante* quantities so as to have some claim to show the genesis of events, can exist only in the mind of an outside observer and not in that of a participant as such. But incidentally we have spelled out in detail an interpretation of the cryptic passages on page 122 of the *General Theory*.*

4.6. *The inducement to invest*

It is in his efforts to explain investment that Keynes's real convictions are most at odds with his formal apparatus. In that ultimate distillation which he wrote for the *Quarterly Journal of Economics*, he comes near to saying this himself. For in truth he did not believe that the inducement to invest could be exhibited as the orderly confluence of other, distinct, definable factors. It was a matter of 'animal spirits', of 'the

* On the foregoing section of this chapter (4.5), Professor C. F. Carter (now Vice-Chancellor of the University of Lancaster) writes: 'To me the missing element which makes the argument [the Multiplier theory] clear is a discussion of the rise and fall of *stocks*. I have always found that the process seems mysterious, almost magical, to students until they have started to think about warehouses emptying or shop-shelves groaning with unsold goods. And it is probably the *stock* at time t which influences most directly the various *expectations* for t to $t+1$.'

In our scheme of the Multiplier process, such as follows a once-for-all increase of intended net investment, the society's total stock of goods of all sorts (comprising raw and partly processed materials, goods ready for sale to consumers and durable productive instruments ready for sale to business men) increases, by production, *during* each income-period and falls, by sale to consumers, *at the end* of each income period, but this fluctuation has no significance and is merely incidental to our method of simplifying the accounts. The total stock of goods is appropriately measured at the end of each income period, when that period's production and that moment's consumption-expenditure have both been taken account of, and this measurement gives the recorded and *ex post* size of the stock. Each such measurement, say at date j, shows the stock to have increased during the just-finished period by $1 - k^{(j-2)}$. This net or resultant *ex post* increment will be made up of a positive increase by an amount 1 in the society's stock of 'producers' goods, the objects of *intentional* investment (mainly durable instruments) and a decrement by an amount $k^{(j-2)}$ of its stock of goods ready for consumers. It is this latter decrement which, in Professor Carter's presentation of the matter, gives business men the clue to increase their intended production still further. But this is also our own account of the matter, for we have assumed the business men to increase, at each threshold j, their intended production by 'the excess of the demand they are actually experiencing at this threshold over their production of the just-elapsed period', viz by $k^{(j-2)}$.

Unquestionably this divergence becomes dramatic, and makes its impact on the mind of the business man, through its visible effect on stocks of goods on the shelves. The matter is greatly illuminated by treating it in this way according to Professor Carter's suggestion. I think, however, that a chief reason for difficulty in understanding the Multiplier process is the failure of almost all expositors of it to explain how extra consumption-spending results in extra employment, namely, that business men react to the extra spending by deciding to increase production.

news', of the tail-chasing endeavour of business men to guess, as individuals, to-morrow's majority opinion to be held by themselves in the mass. It could be treated only as something spontaneous, a law to itself, an inscrutable source of its own mutations. Yet he could not, without confessing defeat, admit that the inducement to invest was incapable of being influenced by policy and of being to some degree administered. What lever could bear upon it? The inducement to invest was the expectation of profits, expected or hoped-for profits were translated into a present demand-price for assets by a discounting process, the rate of discount when altered would alter the result. This rate of discount was the interest-rate, determined in independence of the profit-hopes themselves. Thus if we could not account for hopes of profit themselves, we could perhaps account for changes in the valuation, and hence the effect, of given hopes. There was a danger, not altogether avoided in the *General Theory of Employment, Interest and Money*, that study of the inducement to invest would boil down to study of the interest rate.

We may go further, and claim that of the two basic ideas involved in the notion of investment, the one, that of *time-lapse* and its concomitants and consequences, has largely usurped the place of the other, taking over in large part its rôle and subsuming it under its own. For the second idea is that of *uncertainty*, and although the two are intimately connected, they are quite distinct. We can conceive of an act whose results, in the relevant respects, are known beforehand only to lie in some wide range of possibilities, but which will become exactly known the very moment this act is performed. There being virtually no time-lapse, the main character of such an act would lie in the pure uncertainty regarding its outcome. The unjustified fusion of the ideas of deferment and of uncertainty has perhaps come about through two trains of circumstance. In the first place, in economic affairs knowledge of the present does give us much knowledge of the immediately future circumstances which will surround any act we propose. Thus unless this act is itself so novel in technical character that even a knowledge of its circumstances does not enable us to calculate its effects, we can largely tell what the earliest effects of the act will be. It is only as we look at more distant dates, on whose circumstances the present sheds little or no light because there will have been time for everything to change, that such calculation becomes unsafe and impossible. When we look forward for two, five or ten years we can have no well-founded idea of what inventions will meanwhile have been made, what political events will have occurred and what changes of taste or fashion will have altered the market. It is plainly true that forecasts of the consequences which would flow from a proposed immediate act become worthless as the date to which they refer becomes at all remote: you cannot have deferment without uncertainty, and, however the latter is measured, the two things increase together. In the second place, there has been the historical non-distinction between the reward of accumulation and the reward of enterprise. We shall see in Chapter 6 below that a stock of tools and other material facilities of production can from two points of view be looked on as the physical manifestation of the operation of time-lapse in production. First, time must elapse in order that an excess of output over consumption (each being a flow or time-rate measured in value per time-unit) may build up such a stock, and conversely such a stock can be disinvested into a flow of consumption lasting for so-and-so many days or years at such and such a daily or yearly rate. Secondly, the existence of such a stock implies that the productive activity which goes on with its aid must be looked on as having deferred consumable results. Deferment of the enjoyable results of effort is a disutility for which a price will be exacted, and such deferment makes possible a superior productivity of labour and natural forces so that such a price can be afforded. This would be true, even if the knowledge of how to take advantage of deferment were perfect, so that the need to commit resources today in order to sell goods in next year's markets involved no uncertainty.

We may say, then, that investment (the creation of tools and material productive facilities in general) offers gain on condition of two things: deferment and uncertainty. This gain can be effectively claimed by those who submit themselves to bear this deferment and this uncertainty. Moreover, the two conditions are so intimately related that it is scarcely possible to hope for, or receive, gain on one score without receiving it on the other. For deferment, in fact, involves uncertainty, and uncertainty can only be borne in respect of some stake which is exposed to loss. Such a stake, if it consists of the ownership of material assets, implies that some reward for the deferment involved in the existence of this stock will also be hoped for. Thus it has come about that profit is something both hoped for without certainty and also something deferred.

To say that I am uncertain what will be the outcome of some available action of my own is to say that I have in mind a number of rival conceptions of this outcome, each of which I look upon as in some degree possible. If I place different values on these different conceptions, wishing for one rather than another to prove true, how can I value the action itself which will, if I elect it instead of others, expose me, in my judgement, to something variously conceivable and, within this range, unknown? How can I represent to myself the bundle or range of *mutually exclusive* outcomes all judged possible? Any means of resolving this problem will naturally be adapted to the temperament of the individual concerned, and will thus to a detached observer appear arbitrary. For by the terms of the problem, the person concerned is faced by an ineluctable ignorance, and there is by definition no way of replacing this by knowledge. It follows that there is no one 'correct' solution of the problem. One action, out of several available, must be chosen or will choose itself by default. Each action is equivalent, in the mind of the action-taker, with some one or other bundle of rival possible outcomes. Each such bundle must in some way be valued so that he may choose the one which he values most. Keynes himself leaves this problem untouched and makes no reference to it. His attention is wholly given to emphasizing the fragility of such judgements, their sensitiveness to any change in the fragmentary and incoherent indications on which they are based. There is here a gap in Keynes's formal argument which his reader has in some manner to fill. When this is filled, the formal apparatus is quite capable of reflecting the impredictableness and unmanageableness of the inducement to invest, which is part of the core of Keynes's theme. We come now, therefore, to the description of that formal apparatus and to the question of completing it.

It is an appeal to Marshallian partial equilibrium by the most direct and incisive Marshallian route. At any moment, at each moment (and we are always at some moment or other) facilities for making equipment are limited, and therefore the supply-price of each type of equipment is an increasing function of the quantity of this equipment ordered per time-unit. The demand-price for any type of equipment is that price which, having regard to the profit possibilities it seems to hold and to the interest-rate at which (because available funds could be alternatively lent at this interest-rate instead of being invested in equipment) these profits must be discounted, it is just and only just worth while to pay for a unit or specimen of this type of equipment. By this definition of 'demand price' it will seem to business men profitable to give, in each time unit, just so many orders for each type of equipment as will push its supply-price up to its demand-price. The flow of funds, thus determined for each type separately, can now be aggregated and the total flow of funds being used to buy equipment of all kinds is the determinate investment flow.

The most basic and intractable question raised by this formula, a question which in the foregoing paragraph we have deliberately glossed with the words 'having regard to', is the question how 'profit possibilities', judged with his own private criteria and interpretive tools, valued according to his own temperament, by each individual business man (whether acting independently or merely as one stream of influence on a board) are to be supposed to be reduced to a single demand-price. Keynes makes no allusion to this question in set terms, save in a footnote in the *General Theory*, p. 24, where he says

An entrepreneur, who has to reach a practical decision as to his scale of production, does not, of course, entertain a single undoubting expectation of what the sale-proceeds of a given output will be, but several hypothetical expectations held with varying degrees of probability and definiteness. By his expectation of proceeds I mean, therefore, that expectation of proceeds which, if it were held with certainty, would lead to the same behaviour as does the bundle of vague and more various possibilities which actually makes up his state of expectation when he reaches his decision.

In my book *Expectations, Investment and Income*,* I gave to this Keynesian concept the name of *certainty equivalent*, which has become established in the literature. Keynes here applies it to decisions how much to produce, but it would equally well apply to decisions how much to invest.

Secondly, there will thus of course arise, in principle, as many different *schedules* of demand-price, for each type of equipment, as there are business men interested in it. The ultimate equilibrium price will be that which is low enough to elicit, from all these schedules, enough orders to raise the supply-price to equality with this demand price. Let us spell this out further for the sake of explicit completeness.

Each business man, we may suppose, will have in mind, for the type of equipment which interests him, a schedule specifying, for each of a range of hypothetical prices of this equipment, the number of specimens or units of it that he would buy. That is to say, for each possible demand price he will have his quantitative demand. The suppliers of this type of equipment will, we may suppose, be willing to supply a larger number of specimens or units per time-unit at a higher price. Thus there may be a price which elicits the same demand as supply, and we have a Marshallian equilibrium of the most orthodox kind.

The third question to which we must refer is that of the mutual independence of the demand and supply sides in the market for some individual type of equipment. Marshallian partial equilibrium analysis depends on the supposition that a movement along the supply or the demand curve will not alter the shape or position of the other curve. When the demand and supply are those of a single type of equipment, the same arguments can be applied as justify us in assuming mutual independence of the two sides in the market for a consumer's good: increased earnings of pin-makers will not very much alter the demand-curve for pins. But when we consider the society's total investment-flow, the funds which, per time-unit, it devotes to the purchase of net additions to all kinds of equipment taken together, we have a very different situation. How can we suppose that a change in this aggregate flow, with its multiplier effect on the society's income, will leave unchanged the profit hopes of business men?

* Oxford University Press, 1938.

This leads us to ask whether it was after all expedient to disregard, as Keynes did, the idea of treating net investment as a function of some one or more variables within his system? For if the demand and the supply of investment goods in general, all taken together, cannot be treated as independent of each other, what basis have we for assuming that the inducement to invest will be *weakened* by an increase in the pace of net investment (the size of the net investment-flow)? It begins to appear as if Keynes's 'under-employment equilibrium' may be highly unstable, for a reason different from the sources of instability on which he himself insisted. There may be a tendency, inherent in the nature of advanced economic society, for an initial movement upwards or downwards of aggregate net investment to continue and accelerate in the same direction, carrying the society's income with it. Such possibilities are the subject of the business cycles theories of Harrod and Hicks which we shall examine in the next chapter. Meanwhile we have to consider an alternative (not quite equivalent) formulation of the inducement to invest, and to consider more precisely the role of the interest-rate.

As a matter of pure account-keeping definition, in abstraction from all considerations of date or of past or future, we mean by the *profit* obtained from some piece of equipment the difference, during some time-interval, between the sale-proceeds of what this equipment produces and the running costs which this equipment entails. Let us suppose that the profit expected from some piece or system of equipment is a single instalment G, and that the supply-price of the equipment is S. Then the business man's concern is with the ratio G/S, and this can be expressed in an exponential form

$$G = S\mathrm{e}^{x},$$

where e is the base of natural logarithms. Now if the date of the expected single profit instalment, or the time-lapse which must occur between purchase of the equipment for a price S and the expected receipt of the profit G, were of no consequence, the business man could consider all available investment-projects costing S_j and promising a profit G_j, and compare the numerical values of x obtained by solving the equations

$$G_1 = S_1 e^{x_1},$$
$$G_2 = S_2 e^{x_2},$$
$$\cdot \quad \cdot$$
$$\cdot \quad \cdot$$
$$\cdot \quad \cdot$$
$$G_n = S_n e^{x_n},$$

choosing that type of project which gave the largest value of x. Still maintaining the supposition that the relative dates of paying S and receiving G have no significance, x would then be an analogue of what, for a society where dates do matter, Keynes called the *marginal eficiency of capital*. For if dates do matter, we can say that what matters to the business man is not x pure and simple, but the factor z in

$$tz = x,$$

where t is the number of time-units that are to elapse between paying S and receiving G. Thus we have

$$G = S e^{tz}$$

or

$$S = G e^{-tz}.$$

Under the (inessential) simplifying assumption that all profit comes in one instalment at a single date, z is now precisely what Keynes meant by the marginal efficiency of capital (and what Irving Fisher meant by the 'rate of return over cost', or Boulding by 'the internal rate of return'). When expected profits are to come in many instalments $G_1, G_2, \ldots, G_m$ at the end of 1, 2, . . . , m unit intervals of future time, the expression above becomes

$$S = G_1 e^{-z} + G_2 e^{-2z} + \ldots + G_m e^{-mz} \qquad (14)$$

for which we can still seek a solution, a numerical value of z satisfying the equation and giving a measure of the profitability of the investment-project in question.

Let us take this equation (14) to reflect the thoughts of some particular business man about the type of equipment in which he is interested. Then z is a function of S and of each of the G's, and so long as the latter are unchanged, z is a function of S. For each (numerical value of) S there will be, amongst all the business men interested in this type of equipment, each with his own series of G's, some highest value of z, and thus if we know the supply-function $S(N)$ showing the price per specimen, or per unit, which would elicit a supply of N specimens per unit of time, we can plot on a Cartesian diagram a curve $z(N)$ showing the society's most sanguine estimate of z for each supposed number of specimens of the given type of equipment being ordered per unit of time. Whereas in our previous formulation, we confronted with each other on one hand a supply-price, and on the other a demand-price so defined that it took account of the prevailing interest-rate, we now, by contrast, confront with each other on one hand a profit-rate or marginal efficiency of capital, z (relating to one particular kind of equipment), which already takes account of the supply-price, and on the other the prevailing interest-rate. On our diagram of $z = z(N)$, therefore, we must now superpose a curve relating the interest-rate r to the number N of specimens being ordered. If we take r to be independent of N, this curve $r = r(N)$ will be a horizontal straight line, and so if $z(N)$ slopes downward, the two curves will intersect at some numerical value of N. If we can thus claim for each kind of equipment separately, that the quantity produced per time-unit is determined, we can reckon the size of the gross and the net investment flow for the whole society, simply by multiplying the quantity by the price of each kind of equipment and adding the resulting money values. The net flow will of course be the gross flow less a depreciation allowance depending on the size and composition of the *existing stock* of equipment of all sorts and not on the size of the current flow of augmentations of it.

Again, the difficulties of such a scheme of thought are those of the neglected interdependence amongst its variables. How can the series of G's, which a business man assigns to some type of equipment, be independent of the size of the *general* investment-flow being made by the society as a whole into all types of equipment taken together, as at least roughly indicated to him, perhaps, by the price-levels of equipment of his own and other types? Moreover, if profit-estimates lead to investment and this investment leads to revision of profit-estimates, how can we suppose that all these actions are taken with knowledge of each other so as to bring about an equilibrium? In Chapter 22 of the *General Theory*, called 'Notes on the Trade Cycle', Keynes does in effect consider such a mechanism of lagged responses, but in the body of the book his mode of thought seems to be a quite different one. The function $z = z(N)$ is to be thought of as highly unstable. The equilibria $z(N) = r(N)$ are to be treated as having somewhat the same relation to actual events as the lines of latitude and longitude on a map have to real features of the landscape or the coast. Keynes's *description of what is* goes quite outside his formal apparatus of equilibrium, just as Marshall's description requires an almost Ptolemaic elaboration of the simple basic notion of optimal adjustment, when an account of increase of scale, evolution of methods, and acquirement and exploitation of new knowledge is to be given. With every shift of the news, every report of a canvassing of majority opinion, every straw in the political wind, some fluttering or deformation of the curve $z(N)$ is to be imagined, causing a shift in its intersection with $r(N)$ and thus a presumption of an impending change, upwards or downwards, in the size of the general investment flow.

Now let us ask whether there is anything to choose between the two methods, which we have described, of formally representing the inducement to invest. There is, in fact, one important difference telling in favour of that method which speaks of the demand-price of equipment, rather than of the marginal efficiency of capital. This difference lies in the contrasting ways in which the two formulations reflect a change in the interest-rate. In order to study this, let us revert to the supposition that the whole profit expected from the use of a piece of equipment, which it is proposed to buy, is assigned to a single date of futurity t time-units. If this profit is G money units expected with certainty, and if the interest-rate, one and the same for debts of all maturities, is r per time-unit, the present value v of the expected profit, which present value will be the demand-price for the equipment, is

$$v = G\,e^{-\rho t},$$

where $\rho = \log_e(1 + r)$. It is well known that for interest-rates within a range up to, say, 6 per cent per annum, ρ approximates fairly closely in numerical value to r, and so ρ can be treated and spoken of as if it were itself the interest rate. Now let us see by how large a proportion v will change, when ρ changes by a *given* proportion. The ratio of these two associated proportions, that is, the *elasticity* of v with respect to ρ, will be

$$\frac{\partial v}{\partial \rho}\frac{\rho}{v} = -\rho t,$$

a quantity whose numerical value increases directly with the futurity t of the expected profit, and bears a fixed ratio to that futurity. If, now, we relax the assumption that all the expected profit is assigned to a single date, it still follows that pieces of equipment whose expected profit is concentrated towards more remote future years, will have the present value of this expected profit, and hence their own demand price, affected in a larger ratio by a given change in a given interest rate, than those

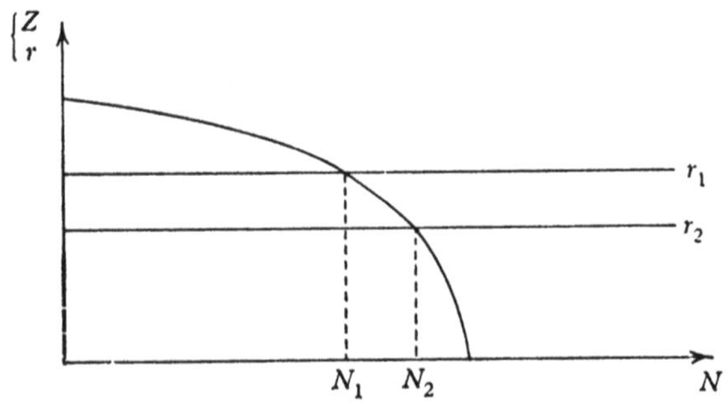

Fig. 4.1

pieces of equipment whose expected profit lies in the near future. In concrete terms, if the interest-rate changes from 5 per cent per annum to 4 per cent per annum, the present value of a machine which is expected to become obsolete in 3 years will be hardly affected, while that of a house which is counted on to yield rents for 60 years will be greatly affected. This principle ought to be reflected in any formulation of the inducement to invest, but not all such formulations exhibit it.

In Fig. 4.1 the downward-sloping curve represents the marginal efficiency of capital, $z(N)$, for investment in some particular type of equipment. The two horizontal lines r_1 and

r_2 represent two alternative levels of the interest-rate. If the rate falls from r_1 to r_2, the equilibrium number of units of the given type of equipment, to be ordered per unit of time, will rise from N_1 to N_2. Where, in this diagram, can we find a place for any distinction between types of equipment which promise large annual profits for a few years and nothing thereafter, and types which promise small annual profits continuing for many years? We cannot find it in the lines representing the levels of the interest-rate, for each rival supposition envisages a given rate applicable to debts of all maturities. If we turn to the curve $z(N)$, we see that its shape must directly reflect that of

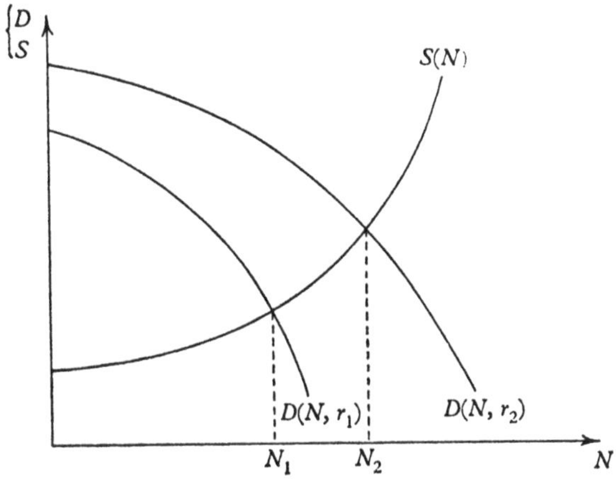

Fig. 4.2

the supply-curve $S(N)$ which connects price of the equipment in question with numbers of it bought per time-unit, and it is plain that the shape of the supply-curve has nothing to do with the service-life, or the economic life, of the equipment. There is thus no means of incorporating into this type of diagram, which confronts a schedule of the marginal efficiency of capital with a schedule of the interest-rate, any reflection of the differential effect of interest-rate changes on equipment with short or long profit-earning life.

In Fig. 4.2 the upward-sloping curve $S(N)$ is the supply-curve of some type of equipment, and the downward-sloping curves $D(N, r_1)$ and $D(N, r_2)$ are some particular business man's demand-curves for this type of equipment, one of them showing how many units of this equipment he would annually demand if the interest-rate was r_1, and the other showing how many he would annually demand if the interest-rate was r_2. The 'shape and position' (let us say the *form*) of each of the two demand-curves depends both on the precise series of expected profits, $G_1, G_2, \ldots, G_m$, which the business man assigns respectively to years 1, 2, ..., m, and also on the rate of interest at which all of these profit-instalments are to be

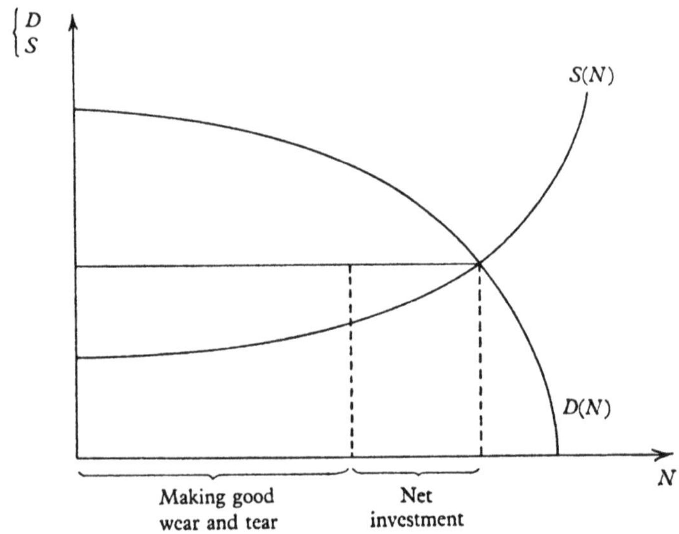

Fig. 4.3

The height of each rectangle represents price per unit of equipment, and the base of each rectangle represents some number of units of equipment. Thus the area of each rectangle represents the value of equipment (of the type in question) bought per unit of time for making good depreciation or for net investment.

discounted. Thus the precise character of the transformation, in the mathematician's sense, by which we can suppose one curve to be carried into the other, depends on the precise profit-distribution over time, $G_1, G_2, \ldots, G_m$. If some remote members of this series are large, or if the series extends far into the future, the effect of a given fall in the interest-rate will be greater than if the profit-series consists of only three or four members in the nearest years.

In representing the formal structure of the inducement to invest by a diagram, a small further advantage can be claimed for the demand-curve method. On this diagram (but not on the other) we can divide the quantity of equipment ordered per time-unit into what is required to make good concurrent depreciation, and what is available as net investment in this type of equipment. This is shown in Fig. 4.3.

Let us speak of a closed governmentless economy. Keynesian theory, glossed in the language of *ex ante* and *ex post*, declares that if there is to be equality between the society's intended saving and its intended net investment, this must come about mainly by suitable adjustment of its intended general output and expected income. For intended net investment being determined outside the system of explanation, and intended saving being a function of expected income, the latter is the only variable whose numerical value we can treat as free to respond to equilibrium tendencies. The older theory, similarly glossed, says by contrast that the interest-rate is the price which equalizes the aggregate of intentions to save and the aggregate of intentions to make net investment, and this older theory further implies that since thus the equalization of saving and net investment requires no adjustment of the intended general output (that is, the expected aggregate income) the latter is free to stand at the level corresponding to full employment, and will naturally stand there because each member of society so adjusts his real wage as to obtain the quantity of employment he desires.

If Keynes's explanation of the possibility of prolonged, massive, general unemployment (a fact of observation in Britain of the 1920s and 1930s) was to cohere in logic, it was necessary to show that the interest-rate is determined otherwise than by equalizing the intended flows of saving and of net investment. We do not propose here to support Keynes's total rejection of the idea of a market where (intended, as we must say) saving, (intended) net investment, and the interest-rate, mutually determined each other. If other forces acting upon the interest-rate could be suppressed, this mechanism would, in our opinion, come into play. The valid claim is that 'the other forces' are, compared with that market, quite overwhelming. The mistake of the older view lay in treating the market for bonds as though it were concerned with flows instead of with stocks. There is, of course, a flow in some sense whenever bonds are exchanged for money. But this change of ownership of bonds is a mere incident in the matter of their change of price. It is more nearly true to say that change of ownership occurs because of change of price, rather than the converse. This condition is the opposite of what prevails in a market like that for fresh vegetables. There the change of ownership is essential and necessary, the market gardener cannot eat a ton of his own tomatoes in a day but must exchange them. The exchange must be mediated by price, and this price will be such as to adjust the daily quantity consumed (that is, *destroyed*) to the daily quantity which ripens. With bonds the situation is utterly different. Occasionally a net addition of a few tens of millions' worth of new bonds is made to the tens of thousands of millions' worth already existing. The stock of money can change by a somewhat larger proportion of itself per unit of time than can the stock of bonds, and changes in this stock of money, as well as expected changes in it, may strongly influence judgements which bond-holders make of the future prices of bonds. But the price of bonds has a unique peculiarity, we may say that it is 'inherently restless', for it depends mainly, almost solely, on guesses about its own immediately future course. Events of some ostensible relevance, like the approaching obligation of the Government to retire one block of debt and replace it with another, or to borrow on longer term in order to 'fund' part of the floating debt, serve rather as the tipping of the dice-box than as compulsive forces pushing the price of bonds up or down. It becomes known that the Government (or some very large corporation) will borrow. The terms are guessed at, taking into account the supposed willingness or unwillingness of the Government to create a larger amount of fresh money. If these terms do not correspond with the prevailing yield of the existing bonds, it will be expected that some holders of the latter will sell, or some holders of money will buy existing bonds at a price nearer that of the new bonds. Thus the prices of all existing bonds will be affected, though only a small fraction will in the event change hands. Almost daily in some periods we may read in the City columns of the newspapers the refrain that 'the changes of price (of bonds or of ordinary shares in companies) was out of all proportion to the quantity of stock changing hands'. What connection do these writers assume between the quantity of bonds or shares changing hands, and the change of prices? If *everyone* suddenly has reason to value a given share more highly, because of some public event such as a profit announcement or a change of taxation, and if it happens that everyone concerned changes his estimate of the value in the same proportion, there may well be no sales at all: the potential buyers who were not quite willing to pay the previous price will still be not quite willing to pay the new price; the potential sellers will be no more willing to accept the new price than they were the old. Yet the price has changed, perhaps substantially. These writers are thinking of shares and bonds as if they were fruit inexorably coming on the market and about to go bad. But this is nonsense. The price of something *to keep* is not determined by the same sort of ideas as the price of something to sell, buy and use *now or never*. With the latter, the size of the flow of the ephemeral goods dominates the market, with the former, the flow occurs only if the judgements of owners or potential buyers of the permanent goods has changed *in different degrees or directions*.

At any moment, in a society such as the British, there exists some stock of money and some stock of bonds. We shall suppose the issuers of all these bonds to be trusted by everyone regarding their willingness and ability to fulfil the obligations under which the bonds place them. These obligations, for any one bond, are to pay stated sums at stated future dates to whomever at those dates will own the bond. It might appear, then, that a bond is simply a stated total of money which will be available in various fractions at a schedule of future dates instead of being all available now. This is the truth, under our assumption of perfect trust in the bond-issuers. But does this imply that bonds and money are interchangeable at some fixed ratio of exchange without further discussion? How, then, would we account for the fact that a bond promises a *larger* total of payments to the lender, than the sum which the lender pays to the borrower in the first place? The *deferment* of the promised payments makes a radical and basic difference, arising purely from that basic fact of the human situation, ignorance of the future. For when I part with my cash to a borrower, I cannot tell for certain when I shall need it again.

If I am going to need it, I shall not be able to get it back from the borrower, for he has promised payments only at *stated* dates, not 'on demand'. The only way of getting my money back will be to sell the bond to a third party, who will thus become in effect the lender. But the *price* at which such a sale will be possible is in the nature of things unknown at the moment of lending. The lender has to bear uncertainty, and to compensate him for this, as well as to give him a statistical presumption that in a large sample of cases he will in fact get his money back in full, the total of future payments promised must be greater than the sum initially lent. There must be an interest rate.

Let us turn for a moment to the arithmetic of the matter. In return for the lump sum which he receives to-day, the borrower gives a promise to pay stated amounts at stated dates. These payments may be equal or unequal in size and their dates may be at equal or unequal intervals. The very fact of an exchange of present for deferred money shows that the time-distribution of receipts and payments, involved in the transaction, is not a matter of indifference to those concerned. Thus in order to compare several differing series of deferred payments, promised in return for equal present sums, we cannot simply take the respective totals of those series. We need a general measure of the price of deferment which a given series represents. Let us write

P for the present sum or principal,

A_1 for the payment deferred one time-unit,

A_2 for the payment deferred two time-units,

—

—

A_n for the payment deferred n time-units

and $$P = A_1(1 + r)^{-1} + A_2(1 + r)^{-2} + \dots + A_n(1 + r)^{-n}.$$

A (numerical) value of r which satisfies this equation will be the general measure we require. Some implications of this formula are useful to us. Let us suppose, for example, that the promised payments are all equal and are to continue for ever at intervals of one time-unit. Now instead of treating r as the unknown, let us take it as given and express P in terms of r. Each promised payment being A, let us also write

$$R = (1 + r)^{-1},$$

$$S = R + R^2 + \dots,$$

so that

$$P = AS.$$

Since r is positive, R is less than unity, and we have*

$$S = \frac{R}{1 - R}$$

$$= \frac{1}{r}$$

and

$$P = \frac{A}{r}.$$

Thus the price, P, which will have to be paid for the right to receive a payment A at the end of every time-unit in perpetuity, when the *interest-rate* is r, is A times the reciprocal of this interest rate. If our time-unit is one year and r is 1/20, P is *20 years' purchase* of A.

We have seen that an interest-rate is a relation between a series of promised payments, each stated as to its date and amount, and the price which at some moment must be paid for the right to receive these payments. The series of payments being specified, the interest-rate involved in buying the right to this series is a function of the price. It follows that interest-rates are determined on the bond market. The validity of this statement has been lengthily and pointlessly argued. It has been urged that an immense list of influences may bear on the working of the market, and the size of the existing stock of money, the prices which are currently being paid for the shares of commercial concerns, and many other things are cited as helping to determine interest-rates. It has even been asked whether it is changes in the stock of money or changes in the stock of bonds that are responsible for changes in the interest-

* By a similar algebraic device to that used on p. 72.

rate. Do Marshall's scissors snip in vain? All the cited influences enter without doubt into the formation of bond prices, but they do so *in the bond market*, and it is in the bond market that bond prices, and therefore interest-rates, are determined.

Every outstanding bond must be held by someone, and all 'outstanding' money must be held by someone. The prices of bonds, of shares and all sorts of assets in terms of money must so adjust themselves, and these various assets, including money, must be so distributed amongst ownerships, that their momentary owners are *willing* holders of the quantities they hold. It is obvious, as Keynes pointed out in the *Treatise on Money*, that when these assets are held as a store of wealth and not for some instrumental purpose like making payments, the main considerations of their holders are, on one hand, what incoming payments these assets earn for their owners, and on the other, and perhaps far more important, what *changes in the money price* of these assets are impending. The money price of money cannot change, but the money price of bonds can, and bonds will only be held by those who believe their prices are about to rise, or at least not to fall considerably. Money, in its capacity of storing wealth, will be held by those who think the money prices of other assets are about to fall. Those who hold this belief, in Stock Exchange terminology, are 'Bears'. Two propositions emerge as a first approximation. One of them is that the prices of bonds, that is to say, interest-rates, can only remain at rest so long as there are *two camps* amongst those who use the Stock Exchange, those who think that bond prices will rise and those who think they will fall. For if everyone thinks they will rise, everyone will seek to buy (though no one may succeed, for the holders may refuse to sell) and the price will be found to have risen; and conversely if everyone thinks bond prices will fall. Secondly, it appears that all that part of the money-stock which is not required in preparation for immediate payments will have to find lodgement in the hands of Bears, for only Bears will refrain from immediately seeking to exchange it for bonds or other assets. We must add, however, that market operators need by no means all be, at any moment, convinced Bears or convinced Bulls. They may be in doubt how the prices of bonds are going to move, and may therefore be willing to hold both bonds and money. Finally let us reiterate the central point, that Bears can be changed into Bulls in a moment by a sufficient price movement of bonds; and vice versa. The price of bonds must move until it has adjusted the relative strength of the Bull and Bear camps, so that there are enough Bears to hold all the 'floating' money.

The result will be an equilibrium in only the most fleeting and transitory sense. The very dependence of a stationary interest-rate on a conflict of opinion means that one at least of those opinions must be almost immediately falsified. If the interest-rate stands still, those who are holding money because they feared a fall of bond-prices are losing the interest they might have had, and may decide to buy bonds: this will cause their price to rise. If bond prices fall just fast enough to wipe out the interest the bonds earn, these prices are likely soon to fall faster, for they are proving a disappointment to the Bulls. So far as small movements are concerned, the interest rate is *inherently restless*.* Paradoxically, it is confined to a fairly definite range, let us say between 2½ and 7½ per cent, by a strong belief that it can never remain for long outside those limits. Such a belief, whatever its 'objective' foundation or lack of one, naturally feeds upon itself. For if, when bond prices rise so high as to reduce the rate to 2½ per cent, there is a general conviction that they can scarcely go higher, no one will be willing to hold them at this dangerously high price and sales will soon bring them down; and conversely when they fall very low, there will appear to be a profit to be had for the taking by buying them. It is in such a context that we can see most clearly how illusory is any attempt by economists to expel from their field the subjective, the conventional, the non-rational, the fruits of the play of imagination.

* This notion and this name for it were put forward in my *Expectations, Investment and Income*, where the argument is more pointedly developed.

CHAPTER V

MODELS OF SYSTEMATIC MOVEMENT: GROWTH AND CYCLES

5.1 *Self-contained and non-self-contained systems*

A *variable* we have defined as a class of measurements which might be made. These potential measurements must have something in common by which they can be identified as belonging to the class, something in circumstance or subject matter which every instance, every member of the class, shares. The numerical result of making or imagining ourselves to make such a measurement is a *value* of the variable. Having in some way obtained or selected a value of some variable, or one value for each of some set of variables, we may know of some arithmetical procedure by following which we allow these known values of certain variables to indicate to us a particular value of a further variable. Such a procedure is a *function* connecting the entire list of variables. The approach to the idea of function may start from a given *procedure*, by which a further, 'dependent', variable is generated from one or several variables whose values are given or known, or it may start from sets of actual measurements, one set for each variable including the dependent one, and may *seek* the appropriate procedure which would summarize the pattern of association of all the variables.

A list of variables considered as one whole, together with any functions connecting some or all members of the list with each other, which we elect to take into account, is what we mean by a *model*. A model is a form of explanation. For it generalizes the association with each other of the respective particular values of certain variables in one particular case or occasion of measurement, and exhibits it as an instance or specimen of something pervasive and widespread in space or in history. Once we have recognized that some collection of people are, for example, playing cricket, or playing tennis, we have in mind a great range of particular actions on their part which will not surprise us, because these actions reflect the rules and purposes of the game. The game, as expressed in its rules, is a model. Each individual action, purposeless and meaningless in itself, makes sense in the light of the whole complex of past and concurrent actions within the game. By themselves human reason and observation do not discover *ultimate* meanings and explanations. What they seek is coherence, and a model is an expression of some structure wherein variables and their changes show coherence and consistency.

A given subject-matter defining a variable can be measured at each of a number of different dates. When each measurement is labelled with its date, a function involving several such variables may stipulate a time-interval which shall separate the dates of the mutually associated values of two variables. Such intervals (*lags*) of various lengths may be interposed between any and every two variables in the function. Thus the function-procedure may instruct us, in order to calculate today's price of some commodity, to use as data the state of affairs prevailing, in one respect, a week ago, and in another respect, a month ago, and so on. If the function has been successfully devised, any and every 'today' can have its price of the given commodity reckoned by looking back the appropriate respective distances in the records of this and that other variable. In such a conception, the recorded earlier values of some list of variables influence the subsequent values of those variables. This is the formal shape taken by those economic models which seek to explain precisely the evolution of a society in its economic aspects. Such 'dynamic' models necessarily involve, in some form and degree, the idea of the governance of the present by the past, and of the future by the present. Lags are inevitably present in such models, explicitly and overtly, or concealed in the nature of the reasoning entailed by an application of the differential calculus when time-lapse is the independent variable. Such models, however, fall into two quite different types. In some we start with a list of variables, and with some set of 'initial' values of these variables, and with a set of functions (equations) associating dated values of the variables with each other, the whole being such that no further information is required in order to know the value of any variable at any subsequent date. These internally complete or self-contained systems are meant to demonstrate with dramatic force and freedom from irrelevancies some powerful principle or mechanism which we may suppose to be present in reality. In reality its presence and working are clouded and modified by countless other linkages and factors which no equation system, simple enough to give intuitive insight, could accommodate, even if these details could be properly determined. Such models in their most precise and uncompromising form are not intended for exact prediction: for only such exactness can be got out of them, as is put into them in selecting the form, and the numerical values of the co-efficients, of their equations. And statistical resource does not yet, and possibly never will, make it possible to be precise. At a more fundamental level of criticism, as we have said above, these models are designed with deliberate omission of all but a single unified mechanism. All that they leave out necessarily threatens even the most short-term predictions which might be attempted with their aid. Such models are tools of insight, not of foresight. And at a yet deeper level, we have to ask whether the very conception of a model which treats the present as wholly and merely a determinate outgrowth of the past may not be basically false.

At the other extreme of the range of dynamic models we have those whose design deliberately leaves out some of the linkages which would be needed in order to calculate the future from the past. A very notable example of such 'open' or non-self-contained models is Keynes's *General Theory of Employment*, where net investment, the flow whose size is treated as the actively dominant feature of the situation, is deliberately left free of any simple determining formula involving only the other 'internal' variables of the system. The whole spirit of Keynes's book insists on the unfathomable subtlety, complexity and mutability of the influences which bear upon decisions to invest. To build a self-contained dynamic model would have been, for him, to contradict the very essence of what he was trying to say, namely, that it is uncertainty, the feeling of a helpless inability to know with assurance how a given course of action will turn out, that inhibits enterprise and the giving of full employment. The desire for liquidity in the composition of assets, the unwillingness, sometimes, to exchange a general and non-specific claim upon resources for highly specialized, 'committed' resources themselves, explains both high interest-rates and a low investment-flow, and itself rests upon the admission that there is no sure calculation of outcomes.

There is in this respectful treatment of the inducement to invest a most striking contrast with the relatively contemptuous dismissal of saving as a mere automatic residue of income depending mechanically upon the size of the latter. And we must not be misled by that imposing vehicle called the marginal efficiency of capital. This is a mere basin in which the investment-decision maker can finally stir together his ingredients, it tells nothing of what those ingredients should be. The marginal efficiency of capital is the mere abstract and general statement of a sum to be done. It entirely lacks any suggestion of the possible sources of the 'givens' without which, of course, no real, arithmetical sum can be done. It really says no more than that expected instalments of profit from proposed equipment must be discounted and summed, and the result compared with the first-cost of the equipment. It says nothing of how the profits themselves are to be estimated, and nothing, either, as to how those estimates are to be adjusted for the flimsiness of any possible base on which they can be erected.

In the nineteen-thirties it was the business cycle, since the second world war it has been the mechanism of steady growth of general output which have offered the most tempting problems for solution by means of closed dynamic models. All such models have been composed of Keynesian elements or at least designed within a broadly Keynesian scheme of thought. We wish in this chapter to examine critically the pre-suppositions, in respect to time, of one example of a growth model and one example of a business cycle model. In Maynard Keynes, Sir Roy Harrod and Professor Hicks there has appeared an English 'dynamic' school of tremendous effectiveness which has preserved the essential character of useful political economy: vast generality of application and incisive simplicity.

5.2 *Harrodian coherent growth*

Self-contained models built with Keynesian component parts (we shall call models thus built 'Keynesesque') had one or other of two purposes: either to explain the business cycle or to show what conditions would have to be fulfilled for growth of general social output and income to persist at some given annual or weekly percentage. These purposes are intimately related, and the first Keynesesque constructor to publish such a theory, Sir Roy Harrod, produced models of both types which were essentially one and the same model. He demonstrated, indeed, that the instability of regular growth, in the sense defined above, would be such as inevitably to throw the economy into explosive expansion or decline. An economy which is bound by its nature to be always flinging itself up faster than the growth of its resources, or down equally violently, is evidently 'cycle-prone'. The resulting sequence of bounces up and down, if we can explain the exact nature of the obstacle at top and bottom and how the bounce occurs, will constitute a cycle. Harrod pointed to the full-employment *ceiling* at the top, and a flow of 'long-range' investment, insensitive to current business conditions, at the bottom, as the means of reversal. Harrod thus provided the bones of a business-cycle theory, but through a desire for a simplicity, generalness and compactness comparable with those of static equilibrium models, he refused to articulate his argument by an explicit consideration of lagged responses, and so in effect asks us to agree that there must be a cycle, without showing us its sequential pattern of phases. It was left to Professor Hicks to assemble the machine in working order and show its principles in detail.

Sir Roy Harrod's *The Trade Cycle* appeared in the late summer of 1936. But one of Harrod's main contributions to the theory of the business cycle has been, according to Professor Hicks, 'his insistence on the propriety, indeed the necessity, of approaching the business cycle as a problem of an expanding economy'.* We shall accordingly start this consideration of self-contained Keynesesque models by studying Lecture Three of Sir Roy Harrod's *Towards a Dynamic Economics*, in which lecture he took up again in 1948, from his *Economic Journal* article of 1939,† the idea of the 'regularly progressive economy'.

The differential calculus was expressly designed to enable

* J. R. Hicks, *A Contribution to the Theory of the Trade Cycle* (Oxford, Clarendon Press, 1950). See pp. 7, 8.

† 'An Essay in Dynamic Theory', *Economic Journal*, xlix, 1939.

flows, that is to say, transformations which occur with time-lapse, to be treated as measurements made at, and referring to, an instant or point of time. The earlier of two measurements is subtracted from the later and their difference is then divided by the number of units of time-lapse separating their dates. If an infinite series of such difference-quotients, obtained by preserving the earlier date but selecting the later date nearer and nearer to it, converges to a limit, that limit is taken to be the time-rate of change of the measured thing at the earlier date in question. Thus though a time-interval is necessarily involved in the idea of a time-rate of change, the measured time-rate or speed is assigned to a point rather than an interval of time. We can similarly measure the acceleration, the pace of change of the acceleration, and so on to derivatives of higher and higher order *ad infinitum*, and these also, though involving by their meaning the comparison not only of situations separated by a time-interval but of the events of successive time-intervals themselves, can by the device of a convergent infinite series be telescoped to apply to a point of time.

We have discussed in Chapter II the idea of action in a time-vacuum, action divorced from the notion of time-lapse. Equilibrium in such a model means merely a set of actions, one for each member of society, taken simultaneously (because we have expressly, and for this very purpose, assumed away the time which might have allowed one such action to precede another) but in knowledge of each other. Artificial and rarefied though this model may be, it enables us to discuss the question how, in real life, there can be action chosen in knowledge of everything relevant to the choice, or some approximation to such a condition. The actions which constitute timeless equilibrium are those which fulfil a set of *corresponding* conditional promises or statements of intention, and these conditional intentions are shaped by the tastes and capacities of the members of the society and the distribution amongst them of possessions having this and that technical character. It is convenient and relevant to our subject to suppose that the actions consist in the exchange of particular quantities of goods, the choice of action being thus resolved into the choice of the quantities. Goods, here, can include services and even productive, that is, indirectly useful services, though a single-moment or timeless system does not obviously accommodate the latter. Such a timeless system is designed for the analysis of one problem, namely the possibility (the logician's or mathematician's 'existence') of fully and demonstrably rational action, action which can be *shown* to be the most successful means of satisfying a given set of desires because the circumstances in which these must be satisfied are fully known to the action-taker as well as to the detached analyst himself. The notion of equilibrium, however, can be used for other problems, and for these it may be necessary to consider the actions as each requiring a quantum of time-lapse. Such time-lapse can be expressed in any units, and the size (length) of the unit is perfectly independent of that of the required quantum, which may be only a fraction of a unit. When an action consists in the production, exchange or destruction (consumption) of a stated number of physical units of some good, this number can be divided by the number of units of time-lapse required for the action, and the numerical result measures a *flow*. If we prefer, then, we can think of the unknowns, or variables, which are determined in an equilibrium, as flows.

Why then, Harrod asks, should we not conceive an equilibrium in which, not rates of flow themselves, but *rates of change* of rates of flow, are determined by certain facts of structure in the society's psychic and institutional being or in its historical circumstances? Despite the suggestion conveyed by the words 'regularly progressive economy', Harrod is really examining a moment in the economy's life, and asking what internal structure of this moment, what set of relations amongst its various groups of decisions and upshots, will be self-consistent and self-satisfying and lead to a repetition of similar growth in the 'next' moment. A moment, not a stretch of time; an event or compact complex of events, not a span of history artificially unified by the detached observer's viewpoint, is what Harrod is concerned with. He says*

I have to ask the reader in what follows to subject himself to a certain discipline, which may not be altogether easy. I regard the fundamental concept in dynamic economics as the rate of increase, just as the state of rest is that of statics. It is the rate of increase that obtains *at a given point of time*, given the fundamental deter-

* R. F. Harrod, 'Second essay in dynamic theory', *Economic Journal*, lxx, p. 279.

minants. In dynamics . . . we are not, according to my view, concerned with a succession of events through time. The analogy with mechanics is, surely, precise. There we seek to determine the velocity of a particle in consequence of the forces acting upon it at a particular instant. Thereafter it may become subject to new forces. The dynamic determinants of economic progress change from time to time, and the consequence of such changes will have to be considered in due course, But, to begin with, we need to determine the rate of increase at one point. This is but applying in the realm of dynamics the procedure so well known, and, I would say, fruitful, in the theory of static equilibrium. It has always been recognized that the determinants of that equilibrium (desires of individuals, etc.) are constantly changing; none the less, it has been found serviceable to establish the equilibrium pattern required by a given set of determinants. I am convinced that we must do this in dynamics also, as an essential prelude to all else. Edgeworth once said of general value theory that 'the path is short, but very slippery'. If this is true of dynamics also, as is surely the case, we must proceed carefully, step by step. One consequence of this method of initial approach to dynamics is that time-lags do not appear in the equations.

Harrod's argument, then, concerns the possibility of growth of the social output at such a percentage per time unit that the continuously emerging consequences of this growth continuously reproduce the conditions which lead to its renewal. The vehicle of his argument is his fundamental equation in its three forms, and it is this that we must now examine.

Harrod's argument involves stocks, flows and accelerations of flow. A stock is stated as a number of physical or value units; a flow, as a number of physical or value units (say, of some product) divided by a number of units of time-lapse; and an acceleration of flow, as a number of physical or value units, divided by a number of units of time-lapse and the answer divided again by some number of units of time-lapse. Let x stand for any unspecified number of physical or value units of goods, and t stand similarly for a number of units of time-lapse. Then a stock is of dimension x, a flow is of dimension xt^{-1} and an acceleration of flow is of dimension $xt^{-1}t^{-1}$. In order to state the size of any flow or acceleration of flow, we have first to specify a unit of time-lapse. This can be anything we like, and its length is totally unconnected with the question how long we suppose the flow in question, or the growth or shrinkage of this flow, to continue. An acceleration of flow is measured by comparing the pace of flow in some time-interval with the pace in some immediately earlier interval. The intervals in question can then be taken shorter and shorter so that a supposedly convergent series of difference-quotients gives us in the limit a measure of acceleration which applies to an instant or point of time. Now in interpreting Harrod's model we shall at first set aside the process of telescoping the intervals in which pace of flow is measured and compared, and shall make this comparison for successive intervals of unit length. Let us name this unit of time-lapse once for all as the *month*, and resolve that throughout our present argument, when speaking of a unit of time-lapse, we shall mean a month. General output, the value, at given money prices, of all the production of every kind performed in the economy in a month, denoted Y, can change in size from month to month. Let Y_1 be its size in month 1 and Y_2 its size in the immediately succeeding month, month 2. Let us write

$$G \equiv \frac{Y_2 - Y_1}{Y_1}$$

and call this the monthly proportionate growth of general output. We here regard the transition from a monthly production of Y_1 units of general output to a monthly production of Y_2 units as occupying one month of time-lapse. We now suppose that the stock of goods of every kind, whose existence at a point of time aids or makes possible the production then about to occur, can also be measured by its value at given prices, and we suppose at first that a given size of flow, Y, of general output requires the application of some given size K of stock of capital goods. Here we are again resolving Sir Roy Harrod's argument into a series of separate considerations which he has preferred rather to drive side-by-side as a team. It is simplest and least ambiguous to rely at this stage on a purely technical interpretation of the accelerator or mechanism of induced investment. We assume that regardless of what 'quantity of capital goods', measured by value at constant prices, may at any time exist, there is for 'engineering' reasons an inescapable fixed ratio between the quantity actually in use and the production carried on per time unit by its aid. We thus ignore two possibilities which a complete argument must later confront. First, a given machine or factory can be worked more or less intensively, more or less continuously. Secondly, when it is a question of creating additional equipment in order to increase general output Y, there will ordinarily be available many different technical schemes amongst which the choice may depend on the interest rates at which money can be borrowed or lent for a suitably long term. For the present we set both these ideas aside and postulate a fixed ratio between equipment in use, K, and output, Y. It follows that when, in the lapse of a month, Y increases by a proportion G, the applied stock K must, in order to make this possible, have increased by the same proportion within the same time-lapse. By what *absolute* quantity does this imply that K will have increased? We cannot answer this question until we know how many units of capital goods stock (measured, of course, in value at given prices) is required in order to make possible the production of one unit of general output. Let C denote this *technically required ratio of capital to output.* Then the stock of capital goods, required in order to make possible the production of Y units of general output, is CY, and the absolute increment of this applied stock of capital goods, required when Y increases by a proportion G, will be GCY. Whence can this absolute increment come from, how can it be supplied? If we assume that the entire stock K_1 of capital goods, existing when Y began its transition from Y_1 to Y_2, was required to produce a flow of general output of size Y_1, then the required increment of K must be *produced* during the month of transition, and must consist of the *unconsumed* part of general output itself. Let this unconsumed part of output bear a proportion s to output. Then if, in speaking of the growth of output, we refer to a past time-interval; if the quantities we name are records of events seen *ex post*; then it follows that this record will show GCY to have been not greater than sY, that is, GC not greater than s:

$$GC \ngtr s.$$

Sir Roy Harrod writes this condition as an equality, $GC = s$ but his argument, up to this stage, leads really to the less restrictive expression.

So far the argument has been concerned with relations, amongst the three symbols, arising from their meaning, which has been that of a description of a self-consistent pattern of events: the mutually compatible growth movements of a just-sufficient stock of capital-goods and of the flow of output which the existence of this stock makes possible. So far we have asked, on what conditions will it be technically possible for general output to grow by a proportion G of itself in a month, given that the stock of capital goods at the moment when this growth begins is fully employed? The condition is, that during this month a proportion s of general output shall escape consumption (that is, destruction) and shall be added to the stock of capital-goods as a net augmentation of it, and that s shall be equal to GC where C is the marginal capital-output ratio, technically determined.

Before we proceed, let us ask whether the term capital-output ratio is unambiguous? We do not here refer to the manifold difficulties of combining in one concept the idea of an immense diversity of technical powers residing in the tools and materials which compose the capital stock, and the idea of assigning to this stock a size expressible in a single number, by which assignment we ignore that technical diversity. Evidently the proportions, in which the stock is composed of this and that kind of equipment, will affect the catalogue of things which this stock can technically do, each 'thing' consisting in the production of some list of goods in some set of quantities per time unit. Nor, as we have said, are we here concerning ourselves with the fact that the technical composition appropriate to one rate of interest will differ from that appropriate to another. We are supposing instead that either the interest-rate remains constant or that its effects on the relative profitability of different techniques of production is negligible. The question we have in mind is a far simpler one. It arises from the fact that a capital-output ratio has, as its numerator, a number which measures a *stock*, and as its denominator a number which measures a *flow*. A flow, however, is so-and-so many units of mass, volume, value, etc., per time-unit, and if we change the time-unit we shall also change the number of physical units produced per time-unit and thus the capital-output ratio. It will be seen now why we insisted at the outset on naming once for all the time-unit to be used. But suppose we express the capital-output ratio as the ratio of capital stock, whose *existence* at each moment is essential to a given production in that moment, to the quantity of production *per quarter month*. The number standing for the capital-output ratio will now be four times as big as before. But since we must now express the speed of proportionate growth, G, as the percentage by which output increases in a quarter month rather than in a month, G will now be numerically one-quarter of its former size. Thus finally, the measurement of time-lapse in quarter-units instead of units will leave unchanged the result of multiplying together G and C.

So much for supply. The argument turns next to demand. On what conditions will the ever-growing general output continue perpetually to find an equal and ever-growing demand? The model (in the form we are considering) offers two sources of demand: consumption of a proportion $(1 - s)$ of general output, and net investment equal to a proportion GC of general output. The ratio u of total demand to general output is thus

$$u \equiv 1 - s + GC$$

and the condition for the whole, and no more than the whole, of general output to be demanded is

$$GC = s.$$

Here the equation is no longer an identity constraining the symbols into compatibility of their respective numerical values according to their definitions, but a condition, which may or may not in any instance be fulfilled, of 'equilibrium in growth'. Harrod draws attention to this difference of meaning by writing the equation

$$G_w C_r = s,$$

where G_w stands for *warranted* growth, the particular numerical value of G which satisfies $GC = s$ when C and s are given.

In what sense are C and s given? s is the proportion which the society desires to save out of any increment of its aggregate income Y over all that range of Y with which we deem our argument to be concerned. Thus s is typical of the psychic numerical particulars which economics takes as given. The particular numerical value of C, in the supposed society we are studying at some particular epoch in its history, is determined by technical facts: machines and materials of specific kinds, combined in specific ways according to the society's existing technology, yield certain physical (i.e. mechanical, chemical, biological, etc.) results. When the market has given us prices for the machines and their products, we have thus the capital-output ratio as something not subject to variation by any choice of the business men, except in so far as faster or slower growth of output may imply a shift in the proportions in which general output is composed of this good and that. When he means his equation to express a condition, an equilibrium of total demand and total supply, Harrod writes the capital-output ratio C_r, intending the subscript r to suggest '*required* capital-output ratio'. But this seems superfluous. C being at any epoch technically given, it will be one and the same no matter whether it appears as part of a self-consistent record of the past, in the *ex post* identity $GC \equiv s$, or in the expression for harmony of the intentions of business men as producers and investors, on one hand, and of income disposers on the other, $G_w C_r = s$.

In thus interpreting Harrod's argument we assumed at the outset that interest-rate changes have only a negligible effect on the relative profitability of alternative known techniques of production. On this assumption the capital-output ratio is independent of the rate of interest. If we relax that assumption, we must modify our statement that the capital-output ratio is not subject to choice by the business men. Under this relaxation, we must suppose that when the rate of interest falls, some techniques which require a relatively high capital-output ratio, but offer economies of labour or other inputs, will become profitable and be adopted instead of those which have been preferred under a higher interest-rate. Whether or not in practice the interest-rate, by changes of such speed and extent as it historically undergoes, appreciably influences the choice of modes of production, this whole possibility is a secondary matter in relation to the main mechanism of self-sustaining growth of output. By 'self-sustaining' growth of output we mean a mode of growth whereby the act of augmentation of the stock of capital-goods which makes possible extra *supply* also

contributes its due share to the necessary augmentation of *demand*.

A very simple diagram will illustrate the foregoing account of Harrod's model. In this model we suppose that in the immediately past short interval the business men have been producing the largest general output that their stock of equipment allows, and that they are now deciding by how much they shall seek to increase this output. 'By how much' means in Harrod's model 'in what proportion', and we have to ask 'proportion of what?' Harrod's model turns upon the dual character and role of net investment, upon the fact that the work of making equipment gives employment and generates income, while the result of making equipment renders possible a larger output for the society as a whole. Indeed, Harrod's whole argument is an endeavour to answer the question 'What can we infer about the growth-path of general output in an economy where net investment is proceeding, from the knowledge that in such an economy net investment has the dual character of influencing the *level* of total expected demand and being itself influenced by the *growth* of total expected demand?' Business men would be able to cope with an expected increase in demand, without investing in extra equipment, if their existing equipment was under-employed. Thus the assumption that the whole stock of equipment which exists is fully employed, is a necessary logical link in the structure of Harrod's model of successful growth. But at *any* particular moment, which we choose as the 'present', i.e. the locus of happenings going on before our eyes, the stock of equipment which exists is a legacy from past history and is hence a datum. Thus the answer to our question as to what the intended increment of general output is to be compared with is: the largest output which can be produced with the existing equipment.

In the left-hand part of Fig. 5.1, where ordinates represent sizes of general output and abscissae represent time-distances from some arbitrary earlier date, the ordinate Y_1 stands for the output obtainable by full use of the existing stock of equipment. Given the size of Y_1, any increment measured *absolutely* and then compared with Y_1 will yield a *proportionate* increase of Y. All our diagram need do, therefore, is to show in absolute terms (that is, as so-and-so many £m. per month per month) the growth implied for general output by the combined weighted intentions of business men. This intended growth is shown by the slope of a line which we may imagine to be pivoted at Y_1 and able to take up such positions as *a*, *b* or *c*. To each such slope, or intended pace of growth, there will correspond some required size of flow of net investment.

Output itself is a magnitude of dimension xt^{-1}, a *flow* measured by value/time. The growth of output is a magnitude of dimension $xt^{-1}t^{-1}$, an *acceleration* of flow, measured by (value/time)/time. The stock of equipment is a magnitude of dimension x, a stock measured simply as so-and-so many units of

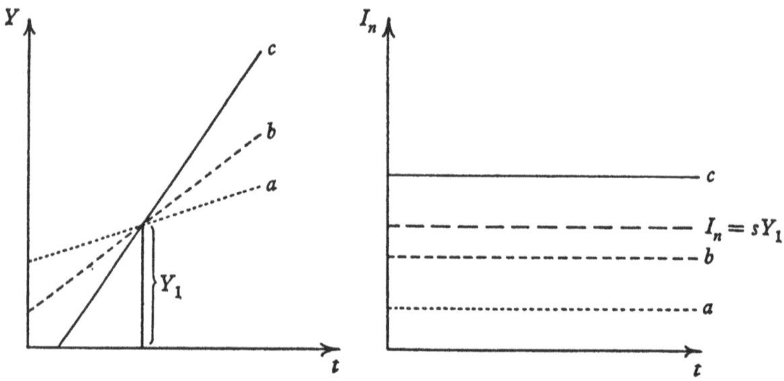

Fig. 5.1

value. The growth of this stock is a magnitude of dimension xt^{-1}, a flow measured by value/time. The growth of the stock of equipment is, of course, net investment. What is required in order to make possible the growth of output is growth of the stock of equipment. To the *acceleration* of the flow of output, there corresponds the *flow* of net investment. The acceleration of output is shown in the left-hand part of our diagram by the steepness of a sloping line, the necessary corresponding flow of net investment is shown in the right-hand part of our diagram by the height (the ordinates) of a horizontal line. For the sake of vividness we may be fanciful and imagine that the rotating of the output line around its pivot hauls up or lets down the horizontal net investment line. But what is the source of the flow of produced objects which constitutes net investment? This flow can only be a part of the flow of general output, a part which is allowed by the body of income-disposers as a whole to be diverted to the building up of the stock of equipment instead of being consumed. Out of any given general output ($\equiv$ aggregate income) they are willing that a proportion s should be thus accumulated. A given proportion of a given output Y_1 (Y_1 is the size of general output which can be obtained by full use of the existing equipment), is itself a flow of given absolute size indicable on the right-hand part of Fig. 5.1 by a horizontal line at an appropriate height or ordinate. Thus we must imagine the sloping output line to be rotated anti-clockwise or clockwise until it has hauled the horizontal net investment line up, or let it down, to the level where it coincides with the horizontal line sY_1, the absolute size of the saving flow from an aggregate income Y_1. This coincidence is the meaning of Harrod's 'equilibrium of a steady advance',* which his equation $G_w C_r = s$ is meant to denote.

5.3 *Instability in Harrodian growth*

So far in his argument, Harrod has sought to show that with given techniques of production, there is one and only one time-rate of percentage growth of general output, at which demand for all products taken together will continually just match their supply. If this matching is taken to be a sufficient condition for the repetition by business men of the same actions as before, we can claim that growth once launched at this equilibrium percentage rate will continue so long as tastes and techniques do not change. If now we release the argument from its sole concern with a single moment and recognize that a moment which embraces change must be deemed to lead to another moment and so on and on, the meaning of a continuing growth of general output at a constant percentage of itself per time-unit is, of course, that the size of output traces an exponential or compound-interest growth-path. Harrod's next purpose is to demonstrate that by departing in the slightest degree from such a path once adopted, business men will create for themselves an incentive to abandon it altogether and to initiate a cumulative expansion or collapse of output. An expansion at a higher percentage per time unit than the one which satisfies $GC = s$ will

* *Towards a Dynamic Economics*, p. 81.

only be possible when the existing stock of equipment is under-employed, so that unemployed machines can be drawn back into use. This fact is the basis of the trade-cycle theory which Harrod originated and Hicks transformed, and to this we shall shortly come. Meanwhile, we have to consider the nature of the explosive instability of growth which Harrod discerns.

Harrod's wording in this connection, in *Towards a Dynamic Economics*, Lecture Three, is liable to confuse. He says

> Taking these two equations together [viz. the two forms of the fundamental equation: $GC = s$ and $G_w C_r = s$] we can see [that] the greater G, the lower C. . . . If G has a value above G_w, C will have a value below C_r. . . . If C has a value below C_r, this means that on balance producers and traders find the goods in the pipe-line, or the equipment, insufficient to sustain existing turnover. Let me repeat: if the value G is above that of G_w, the value of C must be below that of C_r; there will be insufficient goods in the pipe-line and/or insufficient equipment, and orders will be increased. If the value G is above the value G_w, that is if the actual growth is above the line of growth consistent with a steady advance, orders will be increased.

Essentially, this passage is clear and acceptable: In the immediate past, orders from producers to other producers for materials and equipment have exceeded deliveries. These other producers, in their endeavour to increase deliveries, therefore increase their own orders for materials and equipment. Because the existing equipment is already working at capacity, deliveries can increase only in proportion as this equipment grows by the reflux to it of a proportion s of its own current output. But since, by assumption, this takes time, it follows that orders, being unconstrained in their time-rate of growth, will feed upon themselves and multiply without limit. Here we have uncovered both the essential difference between the Harrodian and Keynesian models (about which, indeed, there was no difficulty) and also the unsoundness of Harrod's criticism of Keynes. Harrod says (*op. cit.* pp. 10, 11):

> There is one concept, however, which plays a central role in the *General Theory* which is not static, and that is why the *General Theory* will not be fully satisfactory until it is brought into relation with Dynamics. While many of the restrictions which writers have tried

recently to impose on static theory strike me as vexatious and wrong-headed, there is a more radical restriction which must be imposed but which in fact is less commonly imposed. Positive saving, which plays such a great role in the *General Theory*, is essentially a dynamic concept . . . a steady allocation of one-tenth of income to saving is essentially dynamic, since it involves a continuing growth in one of the fundamental determinants of the system, namely the quantity of capital [capital goods] available.

It is strange that one soaked in the English, that is to say, the Marshallian tradition, should be unwilling to use to its full effect that sharp scythe which Marshall provided for cutting away the entangling stems of problems other than the one under immediate study. What is the *short period*, if not the period long enough for some effects to become noticeable but not others? In more technical language, we have in output, saving, investment, on one hand, and the arrival at a larger stock of equipment, on the other, two kinds of quantity which vanish to a different order. Investment is a flow like that of a stream into a lake. We can take shorter and shorter the time interval over which we measure this flow, and the ratio of the number of gallons to the number of minutes will perhaps converge to some finite limit as we measure over ten seconds, one second, one tenth of a second. . . . Thus we shall secure a better and better approximation to the time-rate of flow *at some instant*, and this can be expressed as so-and-so many gallons a minute. But at the instant in question, the contents of the lake are some given number of gallons. Let t be time-lapse in seconds from some arbitrarily chosen instant, and let $f(t)$ be the time-rate of flow of water into the lake at time t seconds after that instant. Then if t_1 and t_2 are two instants separated by some finite time-lapse, the difference of size of the lake between those instants will be

$$\Delta L = \int_{t_1}^{t_2} f(t)\, dt,$$

and as t_2 tends to t_1, ΔL tends to zero. But $f(t)$ by no means tends to zero as t_2 tends to t_1. Keynes was concerned with employment and 5000 men can be re-engaged by a radio message in a few seconds. But a factory cannot be built in a few seconds. Even if the rate of flow of the stream were instantaneously doubled at instant t_1, the size of the lake *at that instant* would be unaffected.

Keynes was concerned with one problem, Harrod with another, and both of their respective models are legitimate. Keynes cared only for the question what to do *now*, and he answered it by reference almost solely to the effects that rival available actions would have in the present. This may have been unethical, but it did not involve him in non-logic. He wished to increase employment, and he assumed that the existing capital goods would support a more intensive utilization, but only at a rising marginal cost of the product. This rising supply curve of goods in general implied a rising supply curve of investment goods, and thus the schedule or curve of the marginal efficiency of capital represented a decreasing function of the size of the investment-flow, and therefore of the net investment flow. This investment flow could be increased overnight, by engaging some hundreds or thousands of extra men to work the existing equipment, but in a day or a week they would hardly alter the size of that equipment. They would, however, earn wages and spend them, or most of them, on things to eat, wear or burn. Then the multiplier would work, but this, Keynes admitted, would take time to produce its full effect.

Harrod accepted all this, but asked two further questions: First, what determines the strength of the inducement to invest, what lies *behind* the schedule of the marginal efficiency of capital, what governs the size of the prospective quasi-rents that contemplated investment seems to promise? Secondly, what happens when this investment-flow has yielded additional usable equipment? Whence can come the demand for the larger general output that the completion of this new equipment makes possible? Harrod answers the first question by assuming that growth of equipment is necessary if there is to be growth of output, and the second one by showing that if business men, all taken together, take as their test of reasonable future action, not the *level* of output which in the immediate past has been successfully absorbed, but the *increase* of output which has successfully been matched by increasing sales, growth at a constant percentage per time-unit can be indefinitely sustained.

To show what would happen if certain conditions were fulfilled is by no means the same thing as to believe that they will be fulfilled. It seems necessary here to remind ourselves that the condition for steady growth is expressed in terms of the actions of business men all taken together, but they do not in fact take their decisions in common. Each business man decides for himself how much at any date he can successfully invest: his own individual process of investment is a series of spurts with long intervals of quiescence; and there is here no mechanism of conditional promises by which each individual could see his own proposed pace of investment as a contribution to some known total investment-flow. There is, indeed, hardly any ground for supposing that business men all taken together will follow the growth-path which solves the Harrodian problem, the problem of how the Multiplier and the Accelerator can be harmonized. But if they do not, then Harrod shows us, by the highly simplified but incisive mechanism of his model, that they are bound to become involved in a cumulative, self-reinforcing uprush or downrush.

His argument as a whole is plain, but his wording in the passage we quoted seems not quite satisfactory. For he is there treating C as a variable and making its supposed variation compensate for the deviation of actual growth from the equilibrium or 'warranted' growth-rate G_w. C, however, is not a variable, except in so far as it can respond to changes of the interest-rate, and Harrod in the body of his argument assumes such changes away. C is a technical fact and if there is no spare capacity there can be no growth faster than the warranted rate. It thus appears that though Harrod's 'single moment' model of regular growth is well adapted to show how very unlikely it is that such growth can persist, it is not well adapted to analyse the manner in which such growth will break down, if once begun. For that we really need the articulations of 'period' or 'sequence' analysis in the Swedish style, or in the style which we have illustrated in describing the Multiplier process. Harrod seems, in the quoted passage (p. 112) to be interpreting C as the *available* capital-output ratio when G and s are given, and contrasting this with the prevailing, *required* capital output ratio C_r. The model of regular growth along an exponential path is, however, essentially a *mechanical* model, and does not lend itself to the discussion of psychological considerations and effects.

The mechanistic form into which Harrod has deliberately* cast his model raises two particular difficulties of interpretation which we must consider. There is first the question of the meaning to be assigned to Harrod's claim that his 'kind of instability has nothing to do with the effect of lags'.

The student of Harrod's growth model even in its sparest form is bound to remind himself that where derivatives of any order, with respect to time, are involved, there we have in principle a lapse, or several sequential lapses, of time. The characteristic device of convergent series, by which the Newtonian calculus telescopes these time-lapses to an instant, remains the device of the mathematician to give his analytical tools their sharpest edge and greatest ease of handling. But beyond this, we find in the midst of Harrod's model a sudden switch from the mechanistic to the psychic, from a formal structure of symbols to an argument about thought and decision. In *Towards a Dynamic Economics*, Lecture Three, the first statement is that if, in the immediate past, growth has occurred in the output of a society which was already fully employing its stock of existing machines and pipe-line materials, then this growth cannot have been in a proportion per time-unit greater than the proportion: (saving/income) / (capital/output): $G \ngtr \frac{s}{C}$. But next we are to regard the equality, $GC = s$, as a condition for the successful out-turn of *decisions*, and Harrod's wording in some of his publications plainly recognizes this. Business men are to be satisfied with what they have chosen to do, as a condition of their deciding to act similarly in the immediate future. Here plainly we have a sequence of phases, an action chosen by reference to the outcome of an earlier action. Finally we come to the question of instability. If the individual business man finds himself, one day or one week or month, with orders that he cannot fill with no delay, or at any rate, with no more delay than is customary or than has prevailed in the recent past, he will try to increase

* 'The analogy with mechanics is, surely, precise. There we seek to determine the velocity of a particle in consequence of the forces acting on it at a particular instant.' 'A second essay in dynamic theory', *Economic Journal*, lxx, p. 279.

his own output, and to do this he will place more orders than he otherwise would have done with his own suppliers, who will find themselves next day or next week or month, with orders that they cannot at once fill. It is inescapably the case that for the individual business man, in the absence of any centralized balancing of forward demand and supply, or any market equilibrium mechanism for dovetailing the plans of individuals, a shortage of capital stock (or any other shortage) can only appear in the record of what *has* happened, and be adjusted to and legislated for in the decisions about what *is to* happen.

But Harrod admits this. He says*

> [Mr Rose] takes me to task for denying that my theory implies lags, holding that it does imply a lag in the adjustment of the amount of capital to the need for it. I do not deny that. . . . What I was seeking to stress was that my trade cycle theory—if it can be dignified with that name—was not of the same genus as those theories which econometricians were developing with great vigour at that time. . . . These essentially depended on systematic lags between variables in a model which generated an oscillation, explosive or damped.

We can readily sympathize with Harrod's view. It amounts to a demand that we shall distinguish *degrees* of systematicness in models which display sequences of situations. There are models built to an exact quantitative design from which, given the state of the system at time zero, the values of its variables as functions of time-lapse can be calculated. At the other extreme Keynes shows investment to depend on such various and swiftly-changing influences that no equation can hope to explain it, and each situation must be examined *ad hoc*. Between these extremes there are Harrodian models giving qualitative insight into the structure of a very brief span of events, without pretending to extend the relevance of this explanation beyond the 'month' which he judges to be roughly the business man's working interval.†

To an argument thus based on general considerations we can

* 'Domar and Dynamic Economics', *Economic Journal*, lxix, p. 459.

† 'If people find that on a given day, or, to be more realistic, in a given month, they have less capital . . . than they require . . .' ('Domar and dynamic economics', *Economic Journal*, lxix, p. 459).

add one arising from a literal interpretation of Harrod's claim. In an admirable paper* Mr Hugh Rose has argued thus:

But let it be assumed, on the contrary, that current capital outlay is influenced by current events. If there is no shortage or redundancy of capital, outlay will be planned to equal the increment in requirements prognosticated for the immediate future, the prognostication being made by projecting into the future the rate of growth of the firm's output undertaken in the immediate past. If there is a shortage of capital, planned outlays will be larger than this, in proportion to the extent of the deficiency; and if capital is surplus to requirements, planned outlays will be smaller, in proportion to the redundancy.

Using the definitions

- i planned capital outlay,
- c desired ratio of capital to net output,
- y net output ($\equiv$ net income),
- x size of capital stock,
- v excess (positive or negative) of capital requirements over capital,
- s proportion of income saved,
- k a positive constant,

Mr Rose combines his assumptions in the equation

$$i = c\frac{dy}{dt} + kv. \qquad (1)$$

Since capital accumulation can come only from saving, we have

$$\frac{dx}{dt} = sy,$$

and by definition $v = cy - x$

so that $$\frac{dv}{dt} = c\frac{dy}{dt} - \frac{dx}{dt} = c\frac{dy}{dt} - sy. \qquad (2)$$

* H. Rose, 'The possibility of warranted growth', *Economic Journal*, lxix, no. 274, June 1959.

If now we make the crucial assumption that

$$i = sy,$$

we have from (1)

$$sy = c\frac{dy}{dt} + kv$$

or

$$c\frac{dy}{dt} - sy + kv = 0. \qquad (3)$$

'From [equation (3)] it is apparent that $v = 0$ entails $dv/dt = 0$; hence if the economy is on its equilibrium path, it will stay there in the absence of external disturbance.'

It only remains to ask: What *content*, what meaning in terms of human consciousness and action, are we to give to the assumption, which Mr Rose fails to link with anything in his verbal statement, that $i = sy$? The meaning resides in the supposition that 'current capital outlay is influenced by current events'. What are the relevant current events? Surely they are, in the context of Mr Rose's argument, the saving being done by income receivers. In fact, his assumptions amount to saying that business men, having knowledge by some means of the size of the current saving-flow, *will never plan their capital outlay in excess of it*. Two aspects of this proposed interpretation need special emphasis. One is that we must interpret *literally* the word 'current', meaning by it 'strictly simultaneous', otherwise the lag which Mr Rose is expressly concerned to exorcise will be present after all. The second is that in saying 'current capital outlay is influenced by current events' we must mean that there is no lag in *either* of two possible locations. There must be no lag between the occurrence of saving by the income-disposers and business men's knowledge of this saving; and there must be no lag between the business men's decisions to make capital outlay and the actual coming into being of the capital goods. For if the first of these delays occurs, decisions to make capital outlay cannot be tied rigidly to an equality with the relevant available saving; and if the second delay occurs, decisions to make capital outlay are not restrained by their own visible effect and can escape into a cumulative explosion. But beyond these details there is one aspect above all that deserves quite special emphasis: the essential and basic question, here as in other types of claimed economic equilibrium and stability, is that of the *gaining of knowledge*, the question how, in logic and in practice, people can know what they need to know *before it is too late*. The real reason, underlying those matters which Mr Rose stresses and Sir Roy Harrod acknowledges, why growth in Harrod's model is unstable, is because there is (and can be?) no such mechanism of *simultaneity* of action—information—responsive action.

The second difficulty which arises from Harrod's reliance on mechanical analogy is the absence of any distinction in his model between intended and realized saving. '*s* is the fraction of income saved' he says on p. 78 of *Towards a Dynamic Economics*. In order to suppose that the saving flow which actually occurs is equal in absolute size to the result of aggregating all the intended saving flows of individuals, we have to suppose that each individual has had correct advance knowledge of his income. Contractual incomes can be readily assumed to be known in advance and to turn out to be what it was known they were going to be, but not so with the inevitable residual, positive or negative, of the value of aggregate production over the aggregate of contractual incomes. The amount of this *profit* can only be guessed at in advance. What will be the meaning of assuming that these guesses turn out right? In the Harrod model this correctness will be part of the meaning of equilibrium. If business men are going to be justified in projecting recent percentage growth into the immediate future, this also means that their output is going to meet an exactly equal demand, both output and demand being measured in value terms. The value of *output* is the value assigned by the business men in advance, the value of *demand* is the total of intended spending by income-disposers on consumption plus the intended outlay of business men on equipment. Within the value assigned to output is the amount of expected profit. Thus if demand is going to match output, expected profit will be realized.

A model of coherent growth essentially identical with Harrod's was quite independently discovered or invented by Professor Evsey Domar. We may consider Harrod's reference to it in his article 'Domar and Dynamic Economics'.* He says:

* *Economic Journal*, lxix, p. 452.

It is to be stressed that, subject to two relatively minor reservations . . . Domar's equation is identical with mine. . . . One of these reservations is as follows. Domar states his equation in its most familiar form as

$$\frac{\Delta I}{I} = \alpha\sigma,$$

where σ is the potential increase of output per unit of new investment, that is to say $\sigma = \frac{1}{C_r}$ [the inverse of Harrod's required capital output ratio], α is the fraction of income saved, and I is investment. . . . My equation runs

$$G_w = \left(\frac{\Delta Y}{Y}\right)_w = \frac{s}{C_r},$$

where Y stands for income, the suffix w indicates that the equation defines conditions for a steady rate of growth, or a moving equilibrium, and s is the same as Domar's α. The formal identity of the two equations is preserved, owing to Domar's assumption that

$$\frac{\Delta I}{I} = \frac{\Delta Y}{Y}.$$

Harrod's equation tells us that the *existence* of a flow of saving-investment makes possible the growth of output. By inference, if the saving-investment flow bears a constant ratio s to output, the existence of the saving-investment flow makes possible the *growth* of this flow itself. Domar's equation tells us directly that the existence of a saving-investment flow makes possible the growth of this flow. The question that may occur to a reader of the above-quoted passage is whether Harrod ought to have referred explicitly to the fact that if growth of output proceeds along an exponential path, the saving-investment flow will also be growing along its own exponential path at the same percentage per time-unit as output. The answer is that for Harrod's purpose it does not matter. He is expressly concerned with the events of a very brief interval, he may therefore legitimately resort to what an economist may call the Marshallian short period, and what a mathematician of the older style would have called 'neglecting the second order of smalls'. The shorter we take Harrod's brief interval; the nearer, that is to say, we move its end, t_2, towards its beginning, t_1; the less will be the difference between the result, within this interval, of a constant saving flow sY, viz. $sY(t_2 - t_1)$, and the result of a growing saving flow, say $sY(t)$, viz $s \int_{t_1}^{t_2} Y(t)\, dt$, provided the function $Y(t)$ is continuous at t_1.

Harrod's equation has a third form, written

$$G_n C_r = s,$$

where G_n stands for the *natural* rate of growth of output, that rate which allows the labour force, either through its own growth or through the economies of labour achieved by technical improvement, to keep pace with the growth of the capital stock. Real output plainly cannot in perpetuity grow faster than G_n. If, therefore, the investment component of total demand for goods is proportionate to the pace G of growth of real general output, this total demand must necessarily be insufficient for steady growth unless G_n is at least as great as G_w. If G_w is above G_n, growth even at G_n cannot be maintained. For whenever growth is proceeding at G_n, insufficiency of demand will lead to a falling away from this pace of growth, thus to a reduction of investment-demand even below that corresponding to G_n, to a further reduction of the pace of growth and so on in a cumulative slump. On the other hand, if in an initial state of full employment, G_w is far below G_n, involuntary unemployment will appear and quickly grow. These ideas are the basis for a systematization or 'taxonomy' of Keynesian employment theory, whereby Harrod has classified the possible structural states of the economy and shown that to one of these states there corresponds a perpetual tendency to depressed business and to another the likelihood of repeated inflationary booms. On this scheme he has founded a theory of the business cycle of which Hicks has given a more precise and carefully articulated version.

Harrod and Domar (the latter publishing in 1946 without knowledge of Harrod's antecedent publications) perceived one and the same problem and gave to it formally identical solutions. Yet their respective modes of conceiving the problem, and even their technical arguments about it, differ in interesting ways. The problem itself is that of the two-faced character of positive net investment, which is a demand-creator while being performed and a supply-creator when its results emerge. Are the extra demand and the extra capacity for supply required to balance? If their equality is a state equally capable, in logic, of being attained and of not being attained, what circumstance will ensure its attainment? Or if their equality is looked on as a condition for the achievement of something else, what is this something else? Will those human individuals upon whose choice of action the attainment of equality depends, choose that action by reference to the size or changes of size of investment itself, or to the size or changes of size of something else? Is it the 'investment' dial, or some other dial, whose needle's movements they will be watching as their criterion of successful action? Let us use the analogy of dial-watching in another way. If there is one dial registering demand and another registering capacity for supply, shall we assume that the action-choosers can take the mutually relevant readings of these dials simultaneously, or do they do so with an intervening time-lapse which allows them to choose further action by reference to one dial without waiting to consult the other? In the first case we have the Harrod–Domar problem, in the second we have scope for the design of a business-cycle engine like those of Frisch, Kalecki, Samuelson and Hicks.

The Harrod–Domar problem can be formulated in two ways, from the Harrod or the Domar viewpoint. We can ask as Harrod did: What rule must be obeyed if we are to have *unchanging growth* of output, so that our model will be a counterpart of the stationary state which studies an unchanging *level* of output? Or we can ask as Domar did: What will be the consequences of having a positive flow of net investment? For Harrod the primary variable is general output, the primary postulate is that it shall grow. For Domar the primary variable is investment, the primary postulate is that there shall at all moments be enough demand to give full employment. From their respective viewpoints the two writers, save in one detail, reach the same conclusion. Harrod's attention is upon the *size of flow* of net investment and he requires of it two things: first, that it shall be large enough to provide, within the moment or brief interval over which he measures the growth of output, the necessary extra capital stock to make possible the extra output; and secondly, that it shall be sufficient to fill the saving-gap between consumer-demand and general output

(≡ aggregate income) at the current level of the latter. When the moment is brief enough, the level of general output is a given thing whether growing or stationary. There is a paradox here, but it is the old paradox inherent in the nature of the differential calculus. Domar's attention is upon the need for a growing aggregate income to buy the growing potential output of the growing capital stock. The capital stock is growing because a flow of net investment *exists*, but aggregate income can only grow through the multiplier effect of a *growth* of net investment. Thus we must conceive of the net investment flow as not merely existing, at any given moment, at a given level but also as growing at a suitable percentage per time-unit, the same percentage per time-unit as the concurrent growth of the output capacity of the capital stock, and as output itself or aggregate income. Hence Domar's version of the fundamental growth equation:

$$\frac{\Delta I}{I} = \alpha\sigma.$$

Its derivation cannot be better expressed than in Domar's own words:*

[Writing I for the number of dollars invested by the society per annum in increasing its productive capacity, and σ for the increase in this capacity (measured by potential annual production) per dollar invested] the expression $I\sigma$ is the supply side of our system; it is the increase in output which the economy *can* produce. On the demand side we have the Multiplier theory . . . that, with any given marginal propensity to save, α, an increase in national income is a function . . . of the *increment* in investment. Let investment increase at an absolute annual rate of ΔI, and let the corresponding absolute annual increase in income be ΔY. We have then

$$\Delta Y = \Delta I \frac{1}{\alpha},$$

where $\frac{1}{\alpha}$ is of course the Multiplier. Let us now assume that the economy is in a position of full employment equilibrium, so that its national income equals its productive capacity. To retain this position, income and capacity should increase at the same rate.

* *Essays in the Theory of Economic Growth*, Chapter IV, pp. 90, 91.

The annual increase in [productive] capacity is $I\sigma$. The annual increase in actual income is expressed by $\Delta I(1/\alpha)$. Our objective is to make them equal. This gives the fundamental equation

$$\Delta I\frac{1}{\alpha} = I\sigma$$

or

$$\frac{\Delta I}{I} = \alpha\sigma.$$

Finally then, if Harrod's and Domar's respective equations express one and the same argument, why does Domar's equation explicitly involve a growing net investment flow, while Harrod's equation ostensibly contains only the growth of output? It is because Harrod says in effect: *Let us suppose* that output is growing. For this the *existence* of a flow of net investment is necessary. Domar says instead: *We must make* output grow. To do this we must use the Multiplier link between an *increment* of investment and an increment of output ($\equiv$ aggregate income). *Let us therefore suppose* that *investment* is growing. The two theories are perfectly compatible, though it might be claimed that Domar's is the more complete.

5.4 *Shackle's model of a self-generating expectation-cycle*

The second to be published in the line of books containing Keynesesque theories of the business cycle was my own, submitted to the Oxford University Press in 1937 under the title of *The Nature of the Business Cycle* and published in May 1938 as *Expectations, Investment and Income.** Several models are advanced, one of them offering a rigorous theory of the upper turning-point in terms of the 'full employment ceiling', written before the appearance of the *General Theory.*† Theories which rely on different mechanisms to explain the upper and the lower turning-point do not, however, carry to its extreme the idea of a business cycle 'engine' depending for its whole cycle of phases, or its whole pattern of movement, on a single principle of design. One such indivisible, symmetrical con-

* The change of title was made in order to avoid confusion with Sir Roy Harrod's *The Trade Cycle*, issued by the same publisher.

† It appeared in *Economica*, November 1936, and in a further evolved version in *The Review of Economic Studies*, Vol. 4, no. 11, February 1937.

ception was put forward in *Expectations, Investment and Income.* In contrast to those theories which assume or proclaim the business cycle to be independent of the human psyche, it depended wholly on systematic changes of business men's expectations arising naturally from the results of the actions which they had taken in response to their earlier expectations. It depended, in fact, on the Multiplier effect being at first unexpected and later counted on:

Our explanation of the boom by means of the Multiplier effect suggests that the economy's investment-flow continues to grow because each increment of this flow causes a further *unexpected* improvement of emerging yield [viz. the difference between value of output and running costs in a short interval measured backwards from the present moment] of existing items of equipment. But if, when all entrepreneurs have experienced several years of continually rising emerging yields, they become convinced that this rise is going to continue, they will swiftly push up their aggregate speed of investment [the size of their aggregate investment-flow] to the maximum level warranted by this expectation of a succession of future yields each bigger than its predecessor. When, through the Multiplier effect of this latest increase of the speed of investment, an increase of emerging yield duly happens, they will *continue to invest at the same aggregate speed as they have already attained.* This speed was based on the expectation of a continuing rise of emerging yield. The fact that this rise appears to be occurring will not cause any one to make any further upward revision of his estimate of the present value of equipment items which he might construct. No one, therefore, will further increase his own speed of investment, and the aggregate speed of investment will remain at its already attained level. *But this means that, since there is no acceleration of investment, there will be no Multiplier effect.* Emerging yields will fail to rise. The estimates of the value of equipment-items, which were based on the expectation of a continuing rise of yield, will be revised downwards. Many such estimates will now be found to fall short of the cost, at the present high level of aggregate investment and consequent high prices, of constructing the items. The economy's speed of investment will begin to fall, further reducing the estimates of plant-values by causing a reverse Multiplier effect, and discouraging any further development of the equipment-industries. Thus a steep decline of aggregate investment and aggregate income will be initiated.

As soon, however, as the majority of entrepreneurs become

convinced that emerging yield will continue to decline, they will immediately reduce their aggregate speed of investment to the level warranted by this expectation. When this decrement of the economy's investment-flow has its usual and, on this occasion, *expected* Multiplier effect, they will continue to invest at the same speed, but will not reduce this speed any further. This means that the further fall of emerging yield, which would be in accordance with their expectations, will fail to occur. These expectations of a continuing fall, on which their low level of investment is based, will thus begin to be falsified: so far as the present moment has advanced along the time-segment to which those expectations referred, it has revealed something inconsistent with them. Estimates of plant values will therefore be revised upwards, and a positive acceleration of investment will follow. Thus a new boom will be initiated.

The possibility is next considered that expectations might not after all reverse the direction of their change:

In this paragraph we shall have to speak of the increase of the investment-flow *per unit time*, i.e. of the average acceleration of investment over some time-interval, which we may write $\frac{\Delta I}{\Delta t}$, of dimension $ut^{-1}t^{-1}$ [where u is a value unit of stock of equipment, t is a unit of time-lapse]. Hitherto we have assumed simply that if an increase of aggregate income occurs and is *unexpected*, it will cause an upward revision of equipment-valuations, and a consequent increase of the investment-flow; while if, through repetition of such increases of income, a continuance of them in the future comes to be expected, the next occurrence of such an increase will cause *no* acceleration of investment, the latter having been already raised to the level which assumed that this latest increase would occur. But if the belief that emerging yields will continue to rise in the future spreads through the whole body of entrepreneurs in a comparatively short time, the impulse given to investment will be a more powerful one than usual. The increase which the speed of investment undergoes in unit time will for a certain period, following the adoption of this belief, be larger than hitherto. The resulting growth of income and of emerging yields will also be faster than before, and probably faster than was expected. But in this case there will probably still be some upward revaluation of equipment, and the growth of the investment-flow will not entirely cease.

There seems thus to be a possibility that [even if the qualitative basis of the model is accepted] the mechanism will not work, but this possibility is rather unlikely to be realized. For suppose that, in some period following the sudden general adoption of a belief in a persistence of rising yields, the investment-flow increases at a rate $\frac{\Delta I}{\Delta t} = h_2$, and income at a rate $\frac{\Delta E}{\Delta t} = H_2$, while hitherto their rates of increase have been h_1 and H_1. What we have to decide is whether their rates of increase in a still later period, h_3 and H_3, are likely to be larger or smaller than h_1 and H_1. For if H_3 is smaller than H_1, this will be a disappointment of the newly adopted expectations, and will involve a downward revision of estimated equipment-values and an actual fall in the investment-flow. Now H_3 depends on the excess of H_2 over H_1. For income was expected to increase at a rate H_1, and if H_2 had turned out to be equal to H_1 then h_3 would have been zero. Thus unless this excess $H_2 - H_1$ is as powerful an inducement to further increase of the investment flow as H_1 itself was *when wholly unexpected*, h_3 will be smaller than h_1. But since, if the Multiplier is k, we have $H = kh$, it follows that if $h_3 < h_1$ then $H_3 < H_1$. The newly adopted expectations are that H_3 will be equal to H_1. Hence if H_3 turns out to be less than H_1 there will be a downward revaluation of equipment-values, and h_4, the acceleration of investment in the next period again, will be *negative*.

We may put the above more briefly as follows. Provided that the rate of increase of income in a period following the rapid adoption of a belief in the persistence of rising yields does not exceed the former rate of increase by too much, it will still be weaker, as an inducement to continue increasing the investment-flow, than the previous smaller rate of growth of income E when no growth at all was expected. But, if it is weaker, then the rate of growth of I and E in the succeeding time-interval will fall short of the newly adopted expectations, and cause a downward revaluation of equipment-items, this in turn leading subsequently to an actual fall of I.

5·5 *Time-lags within functions*

From the expectation-revision model just described, it already appears that when the effects of action already taken develop slowly; when time-lapse is required to determine what these effects are; and when fresh decision based on these observations again requires time to reach the point of action, we can have a cycle of alternate growth and decline of general output, accompanied by corresponding changes in employment and perhaps in prices. Thus *lags*, lapses of time within the structure of functionally connected events, *can* play an essential part in a model which can explain a cycle of boom and depression, a business cycle. I shall go further than this, and claim that a self-contained model of the business cycle cannot work without lags. It must first of all be pointed out, however, that a self-contained model answers a different question from the one which other theories of the business cycle seek to answer. For in a self-contained model we seek to show that, once an impulse has been given to the system, its natural, inherent and inevitable response consists in a regular sequence of changes of its variables, a pattern of measurements spread through time. Thus in a self-contained model we are concerning ourselves, not with events as such, the superficial manifestation of the system's essential design, but with that design itself as perceived through these movements. In entire contrast with such a conception is that of the search for external causes of first one phase, then another, of a sequence of events which only randomly exhibits the features of a recurrent cycle. In self-contained models we are concerned, as economists should be, with the essential and pervasive unity of things, without which conception 'science' can scarcely claim to be more than a collection of epigrams. In self-contained models we are very little interested in the source of the impulse which initiates the continuing oscillation. The question is, instead, why does this oscillation maintain itself in being in a life of its own, how does each succeeding phase grow out of what has gone before, what is the nature and character of the supposed organic, indissoluble link between earlier and later phases?

We said that a variable is a class of measurements that might be made, or are imagined to be made. How are we to define a particular such class? We can say what sort of thing is to be measured, as for example the general output, stated in value per month at constant prices, of a given nation, or that nation's net investment flow similarly stated. But in some kinds of model we have also to say at what moment those events or situations are supposed to take place, which are the object of measurement. We might elect to stipulate that *a variable* should comprise only measurements of simultaneously occurring events or situations. But it is more convenient to mean by a variable a class of measurements of some given kind of event or situation, no matter when occurring. We shall use letters to name the kind of thing being measured, as Y for a given society's general output, I for its net investment; and subscripts for the date of occurrence, as 1, 2, . . . for the number of units of time-lapse since some arbitrary date called zero.

Now if U and V are two variables, let us suppose that U is the upshot of choices of action made by members of the society guided by what they can see to have been the numerical value of V one time-unit earlier, and that similarly V is the upshot of their actions chosen by reference to the numerical value of U one time-unit earlier. The fact that they choose their U-composing actions by reference to an earlier value of V can be written $U_n = U_n(V_{n-1})$, and the fact that their V-composing actions are based on an earlier value of U can be written $V_n = V_n(U_{n-1})$. Now plainly it can happen (there is nothing in the structure we have described to prevent it) that when they adjust V_n to U_{n-1}, they give to V_n a different numerical value from V_{n-1}, so that U_{n+1}, will be given a different value from U_n, and V_{n+2} accordingly will be given a different value from V_{n+1}, and so on. There is nothing in the essential nature of such a system which ensures its ever reaching a state where a succession of values of a variable are equal to each other, so that those of the other are also equal to each other and we have a 'stationary state'. It is not the case, in general, that one variable can stand still while the other, or others, adjust to it. This variable itself may depend on one or more of those others, and their very attempts to adjust to its value at date n will throw it out of that value when date $n + 1$ is reached.

It will be seen from the foregoing why we had scruples about allowing measurements of differently-dated occurrences to be included in one and the same variable. To allow this enables a variable to depend upon itself. This is a mere question of terminology. It would doubtless be more exact to deny to a class of measurements called a variable the right to have two of its values looked upon as 'alive', 'existent', and claiming attention at one and the same time. For though a variable means in our view a class of measurements, only one member of this class, surely, can play an active part in events at any one moment. But our notation, if not our verbal terminology, makes it clear that when U_n depends upon U_{n-2} (because

$U_n = U_n(V_{n-1})$ and $V_{n-1} = V_{n-1}(U_{n-2})$) we are really contemplating two distinct classes of things. On one hand we have the range or set of values from which, in some sense, U_n can select its actual and existent value. On the other we have the range or set of values from which U_{n-2} could have selected its operative value, which operative value, once known, governs and determines the value of U_n. This last sentence leads us to a second and more important matter. For in it and in earlier sentences we have declared the meaning we attach, in our context of human action, to the *primacy* of one variable in relation to another, to the dependence of the latter variable upon the former. We mean that the dependent variable, dependent in some real sense and mode, and not merely in the formal mathematical sense, is selected by some person or people in the light of the value of the independent variable, which value they take as guide. Knowing the value of one variable, they select the value of the other. This is, of course, an expression of our interpretation of the type of economic model we have called an 'engine'. In the earlier chapters of this book we have shown reason for regarding such an 'engine' as a mere artifice to gain insight into part of the working of reality, for it is a model which, despite our use, above, of the words 'choose' and 'choice', does in a sense exclude the notion of choice in its fullness. Let us remind the reader of our policy of regarding 'cause' as only operative where a human consciousness has selected one of the levers which nature makes available, and used it in seeking to produce desired results. If, as in an economic engine, 'choice' is fully determined by the antecedents or the circumstances present when choice is made, it is difficult to find any useful meaning for the word *cause*. So long as the system is looked upon as self-contained or internally complete, its working is 'all of a piece', not divisible into *source* of events and *resulting* events. All events give rise to others and have themselves arisen as the necessary consequence of others, so far as the model is adhered to.

5.6 *The Harrod–Hicks business cycle engine*

Professor Hicks's book, *A Contribution to the Theory of the Trade Cycle*, clearly shows to the discerning eye the author's mode of work in writing it. A collection of sub-mechanisms or partial structures had been provided by Keynes, by the early Accelerator theorists, and by Harrod. In Keynes's own model there was a curious unbalance or lacuna. He had left investment itself ultimately unexplained, save as the outlet for a natural human adventurousness. He had indeed provided the business man with a sum to do, but he had not told him where to get numerical values to fill in to this sum to turn it from algebra into arithmetic. The *marginal efficiency of capital* is a mere formal re-statement of the business man's problem: 'Shall I, at this moment, spend so-and-so much in buying this technically specified piece of equipment?' What evidence to use, how to interpret it, how to weigh it and combine it, how to allow for its natural, inescapable incoherence and fragmentariness: all these problems were indicated and left unsolved even in principle. Such a state of affairs has been variously accounted for by commentators, some ascribing it to the deepness of the business depression during the years of the *General Theory's* composition, which left so much surplus equipment capacity that the Accelerator could not possibly be at work. More plausibly I believe Keynes would have regarded the Accelerator as too insensitive a gloss on the subtleties, the spontaneities, the imitativeness and wild hopes and fears that influenced the investor in equipment, that daring and tremulous man. But the Keynesesque writers for the most part have been unsatisfied. In contrast with Keynes, they have made their models in some sense internally complete, by linking investment to some other single variable, or small number of variables, already comprised in the model; linking it, not as something determining, but determined by, these other variables. They have, in other words, specified one or two things, rather than a vague cloud of environing circumstances and psychic spontaneities, at which the investing enterpriser looks when making up his mind whether to invest or not; when to invest, and how much. These other things are, for Harrod and Hicks, simply the changes of general output.

Harrod, then, added the Accelerator to Keynes. Hicks examined these schemes and their possibilities minutely before adapting them to a model where some illusions are practised on the reader under cover of a sustained and self-concealing ingenuity of construction and exposition. Let us add at once that these illusions are in fact gratuitous: the author cannot forbear to claim the utmost for his model: infallibility and inevitability: despite some disclaimers; and to support this claim by a sheer virtuosity in dialectic and, let it be said, an occasional casuistry. But his performance would have been impressive enough if he had used in a more natural style the economist's essentially blurred and impressionistic medium, the broad drift of things, the loose sketch of logic, the indication of how some aspects of affairs may work. All 'economic engines' are unreal. Hicks's is needlessly purified of anything which could mar its apparent fatefulness.

Hicks's trade cycle engine has four main component members: the Accelerator, source of instability and cumulative, explosive movements away from the conceptual exponential path of 'warranted' growth at a constant percentage per time-unit; the *lagged* Multiplier, which, not by virtue of its Multiplier action but by virtue of its lags in operation, tends to damp the Accelerator's violent impulses and somewhat stabilize the system; the full employment Ceiling, which stops the explosive movement and, by the nature of the Accelerator, *thereby* reverses it; and Autonomous Investment, which reinforces the increase of production necessitated by the combined exhaustion of inventories and the need to maintain some flow of consumption goods, and helps to initiate recovery. These various schemes do not all owe their presence in the model to one and the same reason. The heart of the matter is the Accelerator–Ceiling–Floor mechanism, which accounts for three of the components and can, by itself, give us a cycle. But the Multiplier is fitted into the total scheme because it is too important a feature of the economic world to be left out. Something must be done with it, and so it is given honorary duties as a stabilizer. But under its other guise, as the Propensity to Save, it does by its particular numerical value affect the critical values which distinguish an explosive from an equilibrium-seeking coefficient of induced investment.

Although the Multiplier has no indispensable role in the Hicksian cycle, Hicks gives it an interesting one in Harrodian regular growth. In Harrod's own model, the required pace of net investment is proportionate to the desired *pace of growth* of output, while the pace of saving (the number of money units saved per time-unit) is proportionate to the *size* of output. Because an output of given size can grow at any pace (that is to say, because the size at any moment, and the pace of growth at that moment, of output are independent of each other), we can at a given moment conceptually increase or decrease the pace of growth of output without altering the size which output has at that moment, and thus we can adjust to each other required net investment and desired saving so that the former precisely fills the demand-gap left by the latter. In this way the whole of output, though bigger at each moment than at the preceding moment, always meets a just sufficient demand. In Hicks's account of regular growth this mechanism of adjustment is interestingly modified by considering that very feature of lagged or delayed response of one variable to changes in another, which Harrod is specially concerned to exclude from his model. Growth of general output Y at a constant percentage per time unit can be indicated by writing $Y_n = (1 + g)Y_{n-1}$, the general output of any period n is $(1 + g)$ times as big as that of the immediately preceding period (compared with period $n - j$, the general output of period Y_n will evidently be $Y_n = (1 + g)^j Y_{n-j}$, and so on). Now Hicks assumes that the society's consumption-spending C_n of period n is some given proportion of its income ($\equiv$ general output or total value added) of an earlier period, say period $n - 1$, $C_n = cY_{n-1}$, so that we have

$$C_n = \frac{cY_n}{1 + g}$$

which, for given Y_n and a given coefficient c, will be smaller the larger is g. That is to say, the faster we suppose the society's general output to be growing, the smaller will be its current (period n) consumption in comparison with its current (period n) income. It follows that when, in the Hicksian construction, we assign to the general output of some given and named period or moment, n, successively higher hypothetical growth rates, g, we thereby increase not only the net investment, I_n, required to be done in this period or at this moment, but also the saving, S_n, which the society will do out of its income Y_n of this period. We have in fact

$$\begin{aligned} S_n &= Y_n - C_n \\ &= Y_n - \frac{cY_n}{1+g} \\ &= Y_n\left(1 - \frac{c}{1+g}\right), \end{aligned}$$

or in more general form

$$\begin{aligned} S_n &= Y_n - C_n \\ &= Y_n\left(1 - \frac{c}{(1+g)^j}\right). \end{aligned}$$

The question thus arises, how are the respective changes of I_n and S_n, brought about by a change of g, related to each other, and in particular, will one of these dependent variables, I_n and S_n, overtake the other, so that they can still be equalized?

To answer this we must consider the Hicksian Accelerator. Writing v for the capital-output ratio Hicks assumes

$$I_n = v(Y_{n-1} - Y_{n-2}),$$

that is to say, that net investment of period or moment n bears a constant ratio v to the difference of general output between periods or moments $n-1$ and $n-2$. In regular growth by a constant percentage increment g we thus have

$$\begin{aligned} I_n &= v\{Y_{n-2}(1+g) - Y_{n-2}\} \\ &= vY_{n-2}(1+g-1) \\ &= vY_{n-2}g. \end{aligned}$$

On the side of income-disposal, Hicks's assumption is that in any period n the society will spend on consumption an amount $C_n = Y_{n-1}(1-s)$, so that its actual or 'accounting' saving, S_n, of period n will be

$$\begin{aligned} S_n &= Y_n - C_n \\ &= Y_n - Y_{n-1}(1-s) \\ &= Y_{n-1}(1+g) - Y_{n-1}(1-s) \\ &= Y_{n-1}(g+s). \end{aligned}$$

The relation between I_n and S_n, each treated as a function of g, can now be represented diagrammatically in two alternative forms. With g on the horizontal axis and I_n and S_n on the vertical axis, we can first treat each of the latter straightforwardly as a linear function of g. In this case, we shall argue that since S_n depends on Y_n and Y_{n-1} but not on Y_{n-2}, we may regard it as unaffected by the change, due to an assumed change of g, in the relation between Y_{n-2} and Y_{n-1}. Y_{n-1} and s being treated as constants, $S_n = Y_{n-1}(g+s)$ gives us a straight line through a vertical intercept $Y_{n-1}s$ at a slope

$$\frac{dS_n}{dg} = Y_{n-1},$$

Y_{n-2} and v being constants, $I_n = Y_{n-2}vg$ gives us a straight line through the origin at a slope

$$\frac{dI_n}{dg} = Y_{n-2}v.$$

Then
$$\frac{dI_n}{dg} \lesseqgtr \frac{dS_n}{dg}$$

according as $Y_{n-2}v \lesseqgtr Y_{n-1}$, that is, according as

$$v \lesseqgtr \frac{Y_{n-1}}{Y_{n-2}} = 1 + g.$$

So long as v, the ratio of capital to output, and g, the percentage of itself per time unit by which output grows, refer to output measured over time units of equal length, we can directly compare them. If a plausible numerical value for the ratio of capital to annual output is 3, and for the percentage increment per annum of general output is $\frac{1}{25}$, it is clear that I_n will increase very much 'faster' as a function of g than does S_n. If the consumption-lag is j periods instead of one, the conclusion will still hold unless j is (in the context) very large. For we should have

$$\begin{aligned} S_n &= Y_n - Y_{n-1}(1-s) \\ &= Y_{n-j}(1+g)^j - Y_{n-j}(1-s) \\ &= Y_{n-j}\{(1+g)^j - (1-s)\}. \end{aligned}$$

When g is of the order of $\frac{1}{25}$, powers of g higher than the first may reasonably be disregarded. Thus if, for example, $j = 3$ we have

$$S_n \simeq Y_{n-3}\{1 + 3g - (1 - s)\}$$
$$= Y_{n-3}(3g + s)$$

and
$$\frac{dS_n}{dg} = 3Y_{n-3}.$$

Since $Y_{n-3} < Y_{n-2}$ and so $3Y_{n-3} < 3Y_{n-2}$ it is still true, with a capital-output ratio $v = 3$ and a consumption-lag $j = 3$, that

$$\frac{dI_n}{dg} > \frac{dS_n}{dg}.$$

The second form of our diagram is obtained by expressing both I_n and S_n from the outset in terms of Y_{n-2}. Then

$$S_n = Y_n - Y_{n-1}(1 - s)$$
$$= Y_{n-2}(1 + g)^2 - Y_{n-2}(1 + g)(1 - s)$$
$$= Y_{n-2}\{g^2 + (1 + s)g + s\}.$$

Again neglecting higher powers of g we have thus approximately

$$S_n = Y_{n-2}\{(1 + s)g + s\}$$

which is again a straight line, this time through a vertical intercept $Y_{n-2}s$ and having a slope $Y_{n-2}(1 + s)$. The two forms of our diagram are shown in Fig. 5.2 (*a*) and (*b*).

In the extremely scrupulous examination which he has given to every proposed component of his model before incorporating it, Professor Hicks has made a number of intriguing discoveries which, however, are not essential to his theme. Some of these, such as the effect of lags on the statistical estimation of the consumption-function, play no part in the model, but others find a place in it, and perhaps the strangest which does so is his special concept of autonomous investment. Strangest of all is the casuistry by which he defends both its presence and the peculiar character he gives it. Some investment must surely be of a kind which has no obvious relation to the growth of output, his argument runs in effect, so for completeness' sake we should

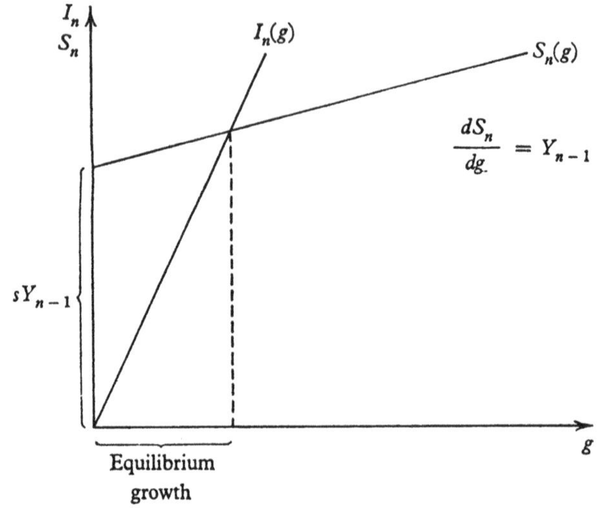

Fig. 5.2 (*a*)

bring it into our model. But of course (the argument proceeds) we must not rely on its vagaries to help in any way to explain the fluctuations in general output which are our problem, for we wish the explanation of these to arise from the logical

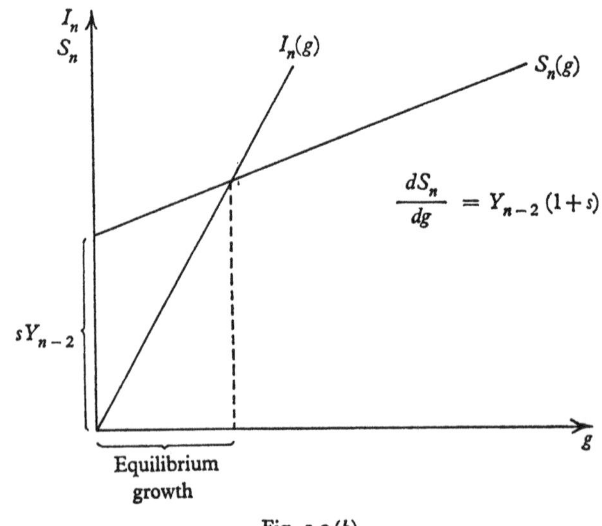

Fig. 5.2 (*b*)

necessities of the model itself. We therefore assume that autonomous investment grows at a constant percentage of itself per unit of time, and in this way autonomous investment can form a part of output in a regularly progressing economy, one whose output is following an exponential growth-path. Such is the plea. It might not be fair to say that autonomous investment is introduced for the purpose of demonstrating in what a peculiar and ingenious sense it may be called autonomous. It is indeed made to play a part in initiating recovery, but it is not necessary for this purpose, and its use here weakens rather than improves the symmetry and self-sufficiency of the model. The main value of the exercise of finding a place for autonomous investment is the light it throws on the nature and meaning of the model-building business itself.

Thus the argument about autonomous investment compels attention to the fact that the model is a manipulation of ideas. We ask, for example, what changes of particular hypothesis will give us a regular exponential growth. Events in the model are of two kinds. There are historical events occupying time, and thus carrying our attention from one particular calendar date to another; and there are structural or conceptual events, consisting in our rejecting one element of its design in favour of another. The two kinds of events are utterly different in nature, yet in describing both we are tempted to use such expressions as 'relative speeds of change'. In our discussion of the question whether required net investment could, by changes in the assumed pace of proportionate growth of general output, be made equal to desired saving, we compared the respective derivatives of these two variables with respect to the pace of growth. Changes in the assumed pace of growth are of course structural or conceptual, and not historical, events, in the context of our argument, and we need to be specially on guard in using and interpreting such statements as 'net investment changes faster than saving does, with a given change of the pace of growth'. Let us imagine a museum bench containing a series of working models of a steam engine. Each successive model in the series represents a further degree in the application of some design feature, such as high steam pressure. Corresponding to each step in steam pressure, there is some particular measured gain in power output. In passing from one model to the next, we might form a ratio of the extra power to the extra steam pressure, and this series of difference quotients would express the gain in power as a function of the increase in pressure. The event underlying this comparison of power and pressure is the shift of our attention from one member to another of the series of models. It is equivalent to a change of design of the model. In contrast with this kind of event, we have the events which constitute the working of a model, the rotation of its flywheel, the reciprocation of its pistons and so forth. The distinction between the two kinds of events is useful and important, despite the fact that both kinds might be exemplified by one and the same occurrence, as when a single steam engine was tried, and its performance observed, first with low steam pressure and then with high.

To understand Professor Hicks's claims about autonomous investment, it is best to start from the fact that we can conceptually choose the size and the pace of growth of general output independently of each other. For this means that with a given and constant numerical value of the proportion of income saved (Hicks's s) and a given and constant coefficient of induced investment ($\equiv$ capital output ratio) v, we can so choose the size and the pace of growth of general output as to leave any desired gap between the saving-flow and the *induced* investment flow to accommodate *autonomous* investment. This gap can be made bigger or smaller, as necessary, by adjusting either the size of general output, which will correspondingly alter saving, or the pace of growth of general output, which will correspondingly alter induced investment. What precise combination of these two means of adjustment shall we (in our conceptual experimentation with various designs of the model) prefer? Our selection will be dictated (hence the justification of 'autonomous') by the pace of growth of autonomous investment, as a percentage of itself, per time-unit. For this pace of growth must be the same as that of general output, or there will begin an immediate disruption and derailment of general output from its stipulated exponential mode of growth. For saving and induced investment are both of them, because of the constancy of s and v, bound to grow at the same pace (percentage of self per time-unit) as general output. The gap between them will therefore also grow at this pace, and autonomous investment is required perpetually to fill this gap precisely. Thus, in sum, given both the size and the pace of growth of autonomous investment, at some particular date, only one size, and only one pace of growth, of general output at this date will allow autonomous investment to fit it. Moreover, within the limitations imposed by the full employment ceiling, *any* size and *any* pace of growth of autonomous investment can thus *conceptually* be accommodated. This fact is the meaning of Professor Hicks's claim that it is truly 'autonomous'.

If, in the course of our conceptual experiments, that is, our procedure of supposing or hypothetically assigning various numerical values for the features of our model, we name the size and pace of growth that autonomous investment shall be supposed to have at a particular date, we *thereby* (through the need to be consistent in constructing our model), name the size of general output at that date. The ratio of general output to *autonomous* investment, given the latter's (constant) pace of growth, is called by Professor Hicks the super-Multiplier. We need to keep clearly in mind the difference of nature between the Keynesian Multiplier and the Hicksian super-Multiplier. When the former is thought of as operating undisturbed by any Accelerator mechanism, the maintenance *in practice* of a given size of net investment flow can be supposed to bring about in practice, when time has been given for the Multiplier process to work itself mostly out, a corresponding size of general output. But the super-Multiplier involves both the Keynesian Multiplier and also the Accelerator, and the effect which the latter will have in practice depends, in the Hicksian model, on the recent history of changes of general output. Thus it is only *conceptually*, that is to say, when we are choosing between various styles or modes of growth which we can adopt for our imagined models, that the application of the super-Multiplier to an autonomous investment flow specified as to its constant growth percentage and as to its size on a particular date, will point to one and only one size, on that date, of general output.

Professor Hicks's quarry is a proof that, in a technologically advanced society, a business cycle is inevitable and is virtually an aspect of the nature of human existence. He stalks this quarry by infinitely circumspect and painstaking approaches from many directions, occasionally having to risk a dash across the open, in the form of a drastic assumption or a brushing aside of a difficulty, done candidly but sometimes with ingenious deflections of the reader's critical impulse. Some critics, such as Mr Kaldor, have questioned the weight placed upon the accelerator mechanism, and it is true that this is the heart and soul of Professor Hicks's construction. As a theory of the inducement to invest, 'induced investment' in the Hicksian sense, more especially viewed as he views it, virtually *ex post*, is crude and mechanical. But this mechanistic character, this certainty and infallibility in action, is precisely the virtue that Professor Hicks sees in it. It is because he desires an *infallible* mechanism that he dares not to use the phrase *ex ante* with its involvement in ideas of uncertainty, of psychic spontaneity, of Keynesian 'high spirited' adventurous investment. The accelerator is his guarantee of safe occurrence of the cycle, and its operation is what we must now briefly study.

Professor Hicks's argument is focused upon a single so-called 'elementary model', either positively in describing this model and its behaviour, or negatively in seeking to show that the various relaxations of its simplicity, which a critic might desire to explore, have little basic importance and can be neglected without essential loss of generality. The model is such that with an appropriate pre-history, that is to say, with an appropriate evolution up to the point where we begin to observe it, it could follow an equilibrium path. According to a first supposition, this path is that of mere constancy of all variables, a stationary state; in a second version, each variable grows exponentially at a monthly or annual percentage common to them all. For notational convenience the equilibrium size of each variable at each date is subtracted from its actual size at that date and the model is expressed in terms of the deviations thus obtained, the equilibrium values themselves being therefore labelled zero. Writing

x for consumption spending,

y for the value of general output ($\equiv$ aggregate income),

$(1 - s)$ for the propensity to consume in the current period labelled n out of the income of the previous period labelled $n - 1$, we have for Hicks's Multiplier

$$x_n = (1 - s)y_{n-1}.$$

Next, if j_n is induced net investment in the current period and v is the coefficient of induced investment, we have for the accelerator

$$j_n = v(y_{n-1} - y_{n-2}).$$

Together they become

$$y_n = (1 - s)y_{n-1} + v(y_{n-1} - y_{n-2})$$
$$= (1 - s + v)y_{n-1} - vy_{n-2},$$

so that the size of general output in the current period is seen as a weighted average of its sizes in the two preceding periods. If now for not less than two past periods y has remained at its equilibrium level, it will continue at this level indefinitely in the absence of some external disturbance.

Suppose there occurs such a disturbance in the form of a spell of net investment not arising from the preceding history of the model but coming as a pure 'accident' from outside it, and suppose that this spell, in itself and apart from any investment which its own occurrence induces, begins and ends within one period, say period k. The general output of period k will thus be lifted above its equilibrium level, conventionally called zero, by the amount, say A, of this casual 'packet' of net investment, and in period $k + 1$, therefore, consumption-spending will be $(1 - s)A$ and net investment will be vA. Following Frisch, Hicks shows that there will thus begin a continuing movement of general output whose basic tendency towards explosion or equilibrium, provided $0 < s < 1$, will depend purely on the numerical value of v. In the elementary model, the critical value of v is unity. If v is less than this, the sequel to our supposed single exogenous packet of net investment will be a 'hump' of induced investment followed either by an unbroken return towards the equilibrium path or by fluctuations of *decreasing* amplitude which will carry y alternately above and below the equilibrium path by lesser and lesser deviations. But if v is greater than unity, either the fluctuations will be of *increasing* amplitude, so that y is carried at successive peaks higher and higher above the equilibrium path, or there will be an unbroken rise of y in a simple explosion. Hicks is content to treat both the latter two possibilities, the straight explosion or the anti-damped fluctuation, as amounting to the same thing. Even if there are fluctuations, the maxima of the path of general output will eventually exceed any pre-assigned level, if nothing intervenes to stop them. But something will intervene, namely, the physical limitation of resources, whose interaction with the Accelerator, causing an inevitable downturn of the path of y, is the reason for adopting the Accelerator in its mechanical form as the sole theory of induced investment. But before we examine this, the question arises of the reasons for choosing the explosive value of v.

The argument by which Hicks justifies his choice of $v > 1$ is, once more, the exclusion of other possibilities because of their failure to explain the cycle. To suppose that throughout the century and a half of industrial trade cycles, v has been actually *equal* to unity, or hardly below it (or, in a model with a more complex lag structure, that v has had the particular numerical value corresponding to unity in the elementary model), would be to invoke a quite special and improbable circumstance. Had this circumstance prevailed, the Frisch mechanism would indeed have given a non-damped, non-explosive fluctuation of general output. But can we be satisfied to say that the cycle results from the *chance* that v has this special value? If not, can we be satisfied to say that a mechanism which responds to impulses from outside itself by a *highly damped* fluctuation will receive such impulses with sufficient frequency to produce the appearance of a cycle? To rely thus upon a very low value of v is in effect to ascribe the cycle, not to an inherently fluctuation-prone mechanism, but to the random disturbances of history: the business cycle with its appearance of regularity and in-built necessity is an illusion. Professor Hicks rejects both these hypotheses, and opts for an explosive mechanism of induced investment, $v > 1$. It is notable that he does so by means of a purely negative argument, namely, that low values of v do not serve his purpose, and makes no mention of a positive argument that would greatly reinforce his case.

For v, which Hicks calls the coefficient of induced investment, is also the marginal capital-output ratio. No statistics have ever suggested that the technical ratio of fully-employed equipment to output, taken over all kinds of production together, could be so low as unity, when output and growth are both measured over one and the same interval of time, as they are in the formula $I_n = v(Y_{n-1} - Y_{n-2})$. A more usually accepted figure is actually three, which would draw from the Accelerator an unbroken explosive upward movement of general output even when s is as high as one-fifth. The question which then remains is whether we are justified in interpreting v as referring to a situation where equipment of all kinds is simultaneously working at that degree of 'capacity' which requires or makes it profitable for business men to match every increment of general output with the full technical equivalent in extra equipment. The constancy which is assumed for v in the elementary model suggests that all industries must broadly be taken as working at the capacity of their equipment, since if different industries were successively overtaken by the need to match extra output with extra equipment, v would increase as y rose from its equilibrium path. In the equilibrium model, therefore, we do seem to be justified in taking the coefficient of induced investment as equal to the capital-output ratio, and as consequently being fully explosive in its effect. Any reservations we may have must be directed at the design of the elementary model itself and its total reliance, when general output is rising, on a constant and mechanical Accelerator.

The second stage of construction of the elementary model has recourse to 'autonomous investment' in the sense described above. A stream of investment, not depending in any way on the growth of general output, is assumed to grow perpetually on an exponential path. Hicks shows, and we have shown by an alternative route, that the monthly (or annual, etc.) percentage growth of this autonomous stream, and its size at any date, can both be 'arbitrarily' chosen by the model-builder, and that provided the natural and labour resources of the economy, in its given state of technology, are sufficient, the size and growth-rate of general output, taking account of induced investment, will accommodate themselves by a super-Multiplier to the chosen behaviour of autonomous investment.

It is at this point in the emerging design of the Hicksian model that the reader's most loyal co-operation is needed. In a brief paragraph and an unobtrusive sentence Professor Hicks requires us to allow that the available quantity of labour and other non-produced resources (the Austrian flavour of the whole Harrod–Hicks construction, in respect of the division of resources effectively into the produced and 'non-produced', has not, I think, been publicly noted) shall increase exponentially at the same growth-rate as that of the equilibrium path itself, which we are now to assume to depend on, and be equal to, that of autonomous investment. If Professor Hicks is shy of invoking coincidence when it would establish the Frischian mechanism as a total explanation of the cycle, it is to be asked why he is willing, at the point of his argument we have now reached, to place upon coincidence so startling a burden. The size, at any date, of the flow of autonomous investment, in relation to the size, at that date, of the population, may reasonably be thought to depend on the strength of the social conscience in a broad sense, dictating the pace at which the society's stock of school-places, hospital beds and modern dwelling units per thousand of population shall be increased. If, at any date, it is felt that the ratio of the annual number of millions spent on these things, to the number of millions of existing people, is not high enough, we may suppose that the flow of autonomous investment will be stepped up, perhaps repeatedly, or that in other words the rate of growth of this flow will be increased regardless of keeping, or making, this rate of growth equal to that of the population. (Let us note once more that it is the *size* and not the *rate of growth* of the autonomous investment-flow at any date that determines whether, at that date, social equipment is overtaking or being left behind by the *growth* of population.) Nevertheless it is only if we require the model to work precisely and perpetually, that we shall require autonomous investment and population (adjusted for advances in technology) to grow at the same percentage per annum. The working of the model could plainly proceed for a time even if this condition was not exactly fulfilled. We ought none the less to notice the contrast between Hicks and Harrod in this matter. In Harrod's terms the assumption, that the available labour force, adjusted for advances in technology, rises from month to month or year to year by the same percentage as the equilibrium path of general output, would be expressed as the equality of natural growth and warranted growth. But so far from assuming that these will become equal of their own accord, Harrod bases his whole theory of business depression or prosperity on their possible, and likely, inequality.

The available labour force, conceptually adjusted for changes in its environment of technology and of supplies of natural forces, constitutes for Harrod and Hicks the *ceiling* imposed upon the expansion of general output. Now if we accept Hicks's resolve to work purely in 'real' terms, that is to say, regardless of price effects, as *compatible* with the explicit and implicit character of his model and its setting, which are those of a highly specialized money-using society, we need not inquire at all about the detailed mechanism of 'collision' between expanding output and the physical limits of this expansion. In physical terms, or in terms of a price-deflated aggregate annual value of production, output cannot, by definition, expand above the ceiling. The pattern composed by the several growth-paths, those of autonomous investment, equilibrium general output, and the full-employment ceiling, all assumed to be growing at one and the same annual self-percentage, but to have successively greater ordinates at any one date, can best be seen by plotting the logarithms of their ordinates against a natural calendar scale. Each of these paths may be represented in its natural form by an equation of the type

$$A_n = A_0(1+g)^n,$$

where A_0 is the ordinate of the curve at some date labelled zero. If A_n is the curve of autonomous investment, that of equilibrium general output, E_n, can be obtained merely by replacing A_0 by E_0, the ordinate of E_n at date zero, and similarly the ceiling can be obtained by substituting its zero-date ordinate C_0. By the super-Multiplier we have E_0 greater than A_0, and Professor Hicks chooses the design of his model such that C_0 is greater than E_0. The rest of the equation is unchanged between these paths, for all three variables are assumed to be growing at the same pace, represented by the factor $(1+g)^n$. Since, for example,

$$\log \{A_0(1+g)^n\} = \log A_0 + n \log (1+g),$$

the picture of each exponential growth curve on the semi-logarithmic scale is a straight line sloping upwards towards the right by an amount representing log $(1 + g)$ per period. Thus the picture which combines all the curves in a semi-logarithmic diagram consists of three parallel, upward-sloping straight lines one above the other.

The reward of Professor Hicks's supremely thorough preparation is the ease and inexorable dramatic necessity with which the complete cycle enacts itself upon this stage. This Greek Tragedy begins with an exogenous dose of net investment. Under the fatal exhilaration of this draught, the explosive co-efficient of induced investment takes charge and sweeps general output up, along a path of growth necessarily *steeper* than that common to equilibrium growth and the ceiling, from the former of these two paths to the latter. Here the growth of general output is abruptly slowed down to the *equilibrium* pace, which, however, only induces enough investment to hold general output on its equilibrium and not on its ceiling path. After at most two periods at the ceiling, general output necessarily falls, and thus changes the character of the Accelerator, which, because of the durability of much equipment, cannot induce *disinvestment* at an unconstrained pace. Durable equipment can be disinvested only by reducing *gross* investment to zero. Inventories of materials being processed or awaiting process or sale can be disinvested at a pace which, at the most stringent interpretation, is *technically* limited only by the speed of the manufacturing process itself. But Professor Hicks seems to slur a little the effect of the disinvestment of inventories on the character of the decline and recovery. He shows that if all equipment were durable, a falling general output would entail a total investment-flow equal only to autonomous investment less the *maintenance* (which is not occurring) of durable equipment. Applied to this flow, the ordinary Keynesian Multiplier would keep general output moving along a 'floor' path lying below the equilibrium path which would be induced by the super-Multiplier. The super-Multiplier will not begin to work again, however, until disinvestment (ordinary wear-and-tear, not made good by any flow of replacements) has eliminated the surplus equipment capacity. When the super-Multiplier again comes into action, general output will rise and the cycle will start again.

In this account of matters, the recovery, that is to say, the fresh climb of general output away from the 'floor', comes about because the *multiplicand*, viz. autonomous investment less the flow of depreciation of existing equipment, is itself all the while rising. There is an alternative mechanism which Professor Hicks seems to overlook.

Even if autonomous investment were zero, a floor for general output would still exist, and it would lie at that level where desired saving out of general output (that is to say, out of aggregate income) was itself zero. For at that low level, the society by spending its whole income on immediate consumption would provide a market for the whole of general output. But even this level of output, to be maintained, would require some minimum of inventories of 'work in progress' and of 'materials awaiting process'. The flow of consumer goods to the retail shops would not stop as soon as the high stages of industry had ceased to supply their products to firms next in line towards the consumer; but when at last the running-down of inventories had moved like a withdrawing tide across the whole web of industry right to the retail edge of it, then the only way to avoid a drop in consumption below the level where precisely the whole of income was being spent on it, would be an increase of production in those parts of the whole business machine most remote from the consumer. And this, like any other increase of production, would be enough, once surplus equipment capacity had been eliminated, to start the Accelerator again.

CHAPTER VI

THE STRUCTURE OF PRODUCTION

6.1 *The anatomy of production*

Productive activity takes an immense variety of forms, most of which depend, for their means and for their purpose, upon each other. Each particular operation is performed with materials and tools which embody the results of many other operations, and helps in its turn to make further objects some fraction of which may serve, more or less indirectly, to make possible the very types of activity that have provided the means of this first operation itself. Productive activities thus belong to and constitute a single whole, within which they are interdependent and from which they draw their means and their meaning. These activities can be distinguished and discriminated with greater or less refinement, so that we get a larger or smaller number of them composing the unified life and business of productive society. To understand society's productive business, and especially to see how this business would be affected by given sorts of event coming from outside itself, and to discover whether it may even have, within its own constitution, evolutionary necessities which will change it without external intervention, we need to break it down into some list of component activities defined according to some principle and related to each other according to some scheme. Total production is a unity in diversity, and we need some model to represent to ourselves simultaneously both of these aspects of the reality.

In such a model, let us suppose that all that goes on in any one work-place is directed to producing a flow of a single homogeneous product, and let us call the business of this work-place and of all which produce a similar product an 'activity'. Our picture of society in its productive business will then consist of a great number of work-places into each of which there will flow supplies of materials and energy of many diverse kinds, each kind the product of some class of other work-places, and from which there will flow out its own product going to yet other work-places which, again, will be of many kinds. It is plain that the activity of each work-place will depend not only on that of its immediate suppliers but, at one or several removes, on that of the suppliers of those immediate suppliers and so on in an intricate network of interdependence embracing the whole society and all of its productive activities. Let us call the pattern of this interdependence the technical structure of production. It is clear that the interruption of activity at any one point or in one class of work-places (one 'industry') would be followed only after various lapses of time by the entailed interruptions at other points or in other industries, and that thus the *technical structure of production* involves also a *time-structure of production.* The recognition of each of these aspects of production may help to explain some economic phenomena and may furnish guidance on how to give effect to policy. In this chapter we wish to consider two methods which have been adopted for anatomizing and mapping the structure of production. The older of these two is the 'Austrian' theory of capital, where the chief names are Böhm-Bawerk, Wicksell and F. A. Hayek: an Austrian, a Swede and another Austrian. The modern method is the *input-output table* of Wassily Leontiev.

6.2 *Capital is time*

Let us imagine two societies entirely similar in every economic respect, and each so organized and equipped that the repetition day by day, by each person in it, of precisely the same operations of producing and consuming as he had performed on earlier days would leave his society's equipment of tools, machines, buildings and bins of materials awaiting further preparation, precisely the same in character as it had been on those earlier days, all wastage in each separate type of equipment being by this repetitive economic life just and only just made technically good. And let us suppose that in one of these societies, in one particular *activity* in the sense we have given above to this word (let us call it activity j) there occurs a strike lasting one day, following which, so far as the physical resources available to him allow, every member of the society endeavours still to repeat the former daily pattern of operations, deviating from it only so far as a change in the tools and flows of materials made available to him by other activities technically compels him to. Now by comparing the size of the output of each activity in Society A with that of the same activity in Society B, in each of the days following the strike in one particular activity of Society A, we can trace the repercussions of that strike through the whole productive system of Society A. First affected will be all those activities to which activity *j* directly supplies its product as one of their means of production. A shortage of this supply may cause them to produce during some interval a smaller output than before of each of their own products, which will thus for a time be in short supply to a further ring of activities depending on those directly supplied by *j*; and so on. Since a parcel of *j*'s product despatched to-day to activity *k* will not be used by *k* until some later day, and *k*'s output in turn cannot in general (unless, perhaps, it is electric energy) be immediately processed by *l*, the *technical* network of paths along which the various activities may be conceived to send their products to each other will be, as it were, projected, in a geometrical sense, on to an axis where the sequential location of activities represents the time-sequence in which they will be affected by the one day interruption in output of *j*. It is plain that an activity, say *k*, will appear several times in such an ordering, for its own output, diminished on one date by the reduction of supply from *j*, may be an essential ingredient for some other of its own suppliers. The picture will be exceedingly complex, but it will still not express the whole mechanism by which an interruption at one point of the productive system, at one particular date, will propagate an effect spreading and re-echoing throughout the system through a long subsequent time. For some of the products involved will not be such as provide the *substance* of other products. When a product *j* does provide the substance of other products, as cream provides the substance of butter, each parcel of *j* is likely to be wholly transformed into *k*, *l*, etc., fairly soon after its own manufacture. But instead of supplying materials for other industries to work on, industry *j* may produce in each day or week one specimen of some long-lasting tool, to take the place, in our stationary economy, of a similar tool which in that week has come to the end of its life.

An interruption in the output of industry j may then mean that one such tool which has to be scrapped will fail to be replaced, and thus the *stock* of these tools may remain smaller, by one item, until the date at length arrives when the item which was never produced would have been due for replacement. At that moment, after one whole tool-life from the interruption of production of these tools, there will be a newly produced tool coming off the production line with no scrapped tool to replace, and the stock will be restored. Thus the effect of the interruption in industry j will affect all users of industry j's products for one whole life-time of these products.

In the apparatus we have been using, any one of the society's productive sectors or industries could evidently be chosen as the one to suffer an interruption. Plainly the time-lag, and the intensity, with which any one other sector would be affected, would in general be different when a different originating sector was chosen. This still leaves it perfectly possible that the time required for a disturbance of given intensity in a named sector k to be followed by the resulting disturbance in another named sector l, directly supplied by k, might be constant no matter where the trains of disturbance had originated, and that this might be true of all similarly related pairs of sectors. If so we can claim that our apparatus reveals a *time-structure of production*, and gives to this phrase an operational meaning which, perhaps, it has lacked in even the modern orthodox formulations of the Austrian theory of capital.

Our foregoing conception of a time-structure of production, and proposed means of revealing it, are however very different from those of the orthodox theory. Instead of an intricate system of interdependent activities, each feeding and fed by many others with necessary materials, the early view thought of each day's output of each distinct kind of consumable good as the result of a series of operations undergone by a separate, individual 'parcel' of 'goods in process' in isolation from all other parcels of the same good and from all other consumable goods, the whole life-history of each parcel, from birth to its ultimate passage into the hands of the consumer, requiring only the activities of human beings and natural forces unaided by any pre-existing durable tools. If the life-history of each parcel from birth to final purchase occupied a hundred days, there would co-exist on any one day a hundred such parcels, each at a different stage of its process of manufacture, one being a day old, a second two days old and so on to the parcel which at a hundred days old was just being sold to consumers. These hundred parcels, echeloned as it were in stage of manufacture, together constituted that part of society's capital stock which was required for the supply of that particular kind of consumable good.

Let us now suppose that each such parcel, no matter what stage it has reached, requires the entire productive power of one man and one acre of ground if it is to advance duly towards completion. And let us call the combined work of a man and an acre for one day a factor-day. Then the parcel which is just being sold to consumers after a process lasting one hundred days is the product of one hundred factor-days. The parcel which at the same date is ninety-nine days old contains the result of ninety-nine factor-days, and so on down to the newly started parcel which contains one factor-day. The total number of factor-days represented by all the hundred co-existing parcels at any one instant is therefore $\frac{n(n+1)}{2}$ where $n = 100$, that is, 5050. Now let us suppose there is an alternative technology whereby the 100 men and 100 acres divide their daily energies equally over 200 (instead of 100) co-existing parcels, so that on each day each parcel, no matter what stage of its transit from birth to consumption it has reached, receives half a factor-day of productive service. The daily output of goods of the type in question, ready to be consumed, will evidently still be one parcel a day. For on the threshold of each day there will exist one parcel which requires half of a factor-day to bring it to completion, one which requires a whole factor-day, and so on down to the parcel which has so far only received one-half of a factor-day: 200 parcels in all. How many factor-days will be stored up in this collection of 200 parcels each at a different stage of production? If we reckon in units of one-half a factor-day, the number of these units embodied in the 200 parcels will be $\frac{200.201}{2}$, that is 20,100 units of half a factor-day each or 10,050 units of the original size and each equal to one factor-day. Allowing for the slight effect of reckoning in discrete units instead of considering the progress of each parcel to be a smooth function of elapsing time, we can say that with the alternative technology, the stock of productive services which have been frozen into the collection of parcels that always exists (keeping its size constant while changing the identity of its composing parcels) will be twice as great as with the first technology.

Let us now take some one identified parcel under the first technology, and write down, for each of the one hundred factor-days successively applied to it, the number of days which have to elapse between that application and the completion of the parcel. The list will be as follows:

first factor-day	100 days to completion
second factor-day	99 days to completion
...	...
hundredth factor-day	1 day to completion
Total:	5050 days

[We could with equal justice use a list beginning with 99 days and ending with 0 days, thus getting a total of 4950 days. This looseness in the reckoning arises from our treating factor-services as applied in discrete instalments instead of in a time-continuous stream.] Dividing the total by the number of factor-days applied to the parcel, we get an *average period of production* of 50 days approximately. A similar calculation for the second technology gives an average period of production of approximately 100 days. It is plain that the average period of production, thus defined, is merely another way of expressing the size of the stock of goods represented by the entire collection of parcels required at all times to exist when one or the other technology is in full operation. For the first technology we require at all times a collection of 100 parcels representing altogether 5050 applied factor-days. For the second technology we require 200 parcels representing altogether 10,050 applied factor-days. Doubling the size of the stock, measured by the number of applied factor-days it incorporates, means doubling the average period of production, and vice versa. It is, perhaps, intuitively plain also that a similar proposition would hold even if the application of factor-days of productive service to any one parcel proceeded at a varying speed, instead of a uniform speed as we have supposed.

The mere mechanical framework which, under the subheading *Capital is time*, we have now constructed for Böhm-Bawerk's theory, does not make it plain why we spoke of two *technologies*. It would indeed be technically possible for the production of some good to be organized so as to use a smaller or a larger stock of partly processed materials, without there being any difference between the two kinds of process in the technical methods used. But to use a larger stock of partly processed materials would in such a case be economically pointless, and even disadvantageous, for at the very least it would require more space for the housing of this larger stock. The point of Böhm-Bawerk's theory is that the use of a larger stock, or as we can equally well say, of a longer average period of production, makes possible a more efficient technology. If, in a given state of technical knowledge, we were able to review all possible technically distinct procedures for making some defined product, there would for many a product be some procedures where the spreading of work over a greater span of time would yield, in the end, more product for a given total input of the services of labour and natural forces. An example often quoted is that of forestry, where if we suppose that land and natural forces are free, and that the only labour required in a forest is to sow acorns or beech nuts, then the longer the forester waits for his trees to grow, the heavier they will be without further exertion on his part. This is a poor example even within its own assumptions, for plainly the growth of the trees is due to natural forces, and to assume that these are free, so that for example the land occupied by the forest has no other possible use, is an evasion of the problem. The important and powerful kind of explanation for the possibility of economizing labour and natural forces by using up more time between input and output, is that this extra time allows us to make specialized tools and, in general, to practise the division of labour. This explanation applies with far greater conviction when we look at the realistic model where different industries supply each other with partly processed materials in an intricate pattern of interdependence, than if we use the primitive Austrian conception of separate non-interacting processes. For in this more complex picture, a relatively long average period of production will be the consequence chiefly of the extensive use of durable tools. It is the durability of much of the technical apparatus used by an advanced society, the durability of its machines and buildings, which mainly interposes a long average delay between the doing of work and the gathering, by society as a whole, of some desirable result ascribable to that work. But it is also this durability of tools which makes it impossible to ascribe unequivocally a given day's output of finished consumers' goods to the particular exertions of a given earlier day or days.

Let us return, then, to Böhm-Bawerk's model where certain questions which we must now attack can be argued out in detail. The chief of these questions are as follows:

(i) If *given* quantities of human and natural forces can yield a larger product by being deployed in ways which require a longer wait, on the average, between their application and the result, what is the physical or technical manifestation of 'time as an instrument'?

(ii) How does the existence of this instrument yield an income, and how does that income come to have a particular size?

(iii) Who creates, and therefore owns, this instrument and receives what it earns?

(iv) Why does not the superior productivity of time-consuming methods lead to an indefinite extension of the average period of production?

(v) What questions can be answered or what insight gained by looking upon the pure lapse of time as an influence on the efficiency of factors of production or even as itself a factor of production?

We have already answered the first of these questions. It is plain that the activity of an earlier day can only assist that of a later day if some vehicle carries forward the earlier day's results. The earlier day must leave its mark on the environment and this mark must somehow be transmitted, either by the making of some durable instrument or by setting in motion a train of operations, each earlier one aiding the next until the final day and its desired result are achieved. The material objects which have been moved, shaped or assembled on earlier days so that they serve the purposes of later days are capital equipment. The characteristics which have been deliberately given to them, to enable them to serve further productive purposes, are valuable, and it is these qualities of these objects which physically embody 'time as an instrument of production'. We saw that there is a correspondence or association between the length of the average period of production and the quantity of factor-days stored up in the collection of 'parcels' whose continuous, moment-to-moment, permanent existence is a necessary condition of the given productive technique. A longer period of production implies a larger collection of parcels, that is, a larger, and more valuable, capital stock. It is this capital stock or equipment which mediates and manifests the pure role of time in production.

This conclusion itself leads on to our question (v): What is gained by interpreting a large stock of equipment as the manifestation of a long average period elapsing between mutually associated inputs and outputs? And further, can we not draw from the conclusion that 'capital is time and time is capital' an answer to our fourth question? For we regard the 'law of diminishing productivity' as applying to all the 'natural', non-produced, factors of production, that is to say, to all forms of labour and of natural forces. If we compare the annual product of 500 acres and 10 men with that of 500 acres and 11 men, or 12 men, and so on, we expect that at some stage the presence of an nth man will make less difference than was made by the presence of an $(n-1)^{th}$ man, and so on. Why should not a similar principle apply to equipment? It is indeed implicit in Böhm-Bawerk's construction, that we are discussing a society with a *given* stock of knowledge, and a society therefore which has a given reservoir of technical possibilities for improving the productivity of labour and natural forces. How will it choose amongst the available technologies?

Let us suppose a list to be made of these technologies in increasing order of the quantity of product which each of them obtains from a given number of factor-days. (If we prefer, we can say 'from the work of one man on one acre for one day'.) And now suppose that from this list we strike out every technology which requires a longer average period of production, a longer wait for the product attributable to a given day's labour, than some technology which offers an equal or greater economy, a larger product per factor-day. In the list thus refined, each successive item will offer a larger product per factor-day at the cost of a longer average period of production. Now we have already invoked an argument to suggest that the increase in the product will not, beyond some point in the list, keep pace with the increase in the period of production. For this latter increase corresponds to, and can be interpreted as, an increase in the size of stock of capital equipment, and this stock, we have suggested, can be looked on as a factor of production subject, like all others, to diminishing marginal productivity. Thus we must suppose that, beyond some point in the list, greater economy of the services of labour and land can be secured only by a longer wait for each unit of product. It would not serve the purpose of our search for the criterion of an 'equilibrium' technology to claim merely that a more productive technology would require a longer wait between input and attributable output, for its greater productivity might outweigh the longer wait, so that the 'wait per unit' might actually be reduced. The argument is not rigorous: but the law of diminishing productivity itself, in its ordinary applications, depends on a *reductio ad absurdum* and not on a constructive proof. We must be content, as so often in economic theory, with an argument which appeals partly to experience of how the natural world 'happens' to be organized.

One further assumption is needed: that the members of the society are not indifferent about the degree of postponement of the results of given efforts. If, being able to assign the consumable results of today's work to particular future dates, they prefer to have these products earlier rather than later, they will find that one particular technology gives them a preferred balance between economy of labour-land services, on one hand, and economy of postponement, on the other. It is the old story of maximizing satisfaction by balancing marginal advantages or disadvantages.

We are left with questions (ii) and (iii): Who creates the capital stock, how does its existence yield an income, and how does that income come to have a particular size? These are the questions which Böhm-Bawerk's whole construction was designed to answer. How, then, did the capital stock come into being? If the size of the capital stock can be measured by the length of the average period of production, it is plain that the growth of that stock from small beginnings implies a growth of the average period of production. People, that is to say, who could have eaten up today the whole fruit of their labour of today, must be willing to postpone that eating. But to work without consuming is to save. Savings belong to those who make the sacrifice or perform the necessary abstention, and thus the ownership of the capital stock derives from an ability and willingness to consume, during some period, less than is produced in that period. It is not a long, but a steadily lengthening, period of production that involves saving. It is also true, indeed, that the preservation of the material basis of a highly efficient technology requires an abstention from *dis*-saving. It is because its existence permits the use of a technology which gives more product per unit of labour and land, that a capital stock, brought into existence by saving and preserved by abstention from dis-saving, yields an income. The size of that income, in a society with given knowledge, will depend on how far they have pushed out the margin of exploitation of the list of available and successively more efficient and successively more capital-requiring, that is, time-requiring, technologies. Diminishing marginal productivity of the capital stock, or if we prefer, of the average period of production, offers a smaller and smaller reward to given extra quantities of capital accumulation. If the unwillingness to provide these equal successive quantities is constant, or actually increasing, there will therefore be a point of balance between increase in product and increase in sacrifice, and there the marginal product of capital stock, or of time in production, will take one particular value and thus determine the share of the total product which can be claimed by the owners of the capital stock.

The Austrian theory is essentially non-monetary. It proceeds as though referring to a society where money fills no role except that of a unit of account. All the other capacities of money, such as making possible the sale of goods without a concurrent purchase, and of serving as an asset whose price cannot change in terms of money and which thus provides an escape from the fear of falling money prices of other assets, are entirely set aside. Thus an income derived from the possession of wealth cannot be ascribed by the Austrian theory to any qualities of money, and must be explained by 'real' characteristics of economic life. The real characteristics which it invokes are, first, the power of a capital stock (that is, a stock of real goods serving by their existence to aid production) to increase the product of given quantities of labour and land; and secondly, the fact that the creation and the maintenance in being of such a stock implies the building up and the maintenance of a time-gap between the performance of productive service and the reaping and enjoyment of its consumable fruits, a gap which is distasteful to impatient humanity and which renders a capital stock a scarce means of production. Scarcity implies market value. Those who can offer the services of a capital stock can therefore get pay for the use of it, and it is the nature, justification and determination of this pay which Böhm-Bawerk and his successors have sought by their theory to investigate and explain.

The idea that the immensely heterogeneous collection of items which make up the capital stock, the equipment, of a modern society, could be reduced to virtual and even operational homogeneity by being seen as the physical manifestation of the part played in production by time, is at first sight arresting and illuminating. All that we have said in the foregoing part of this chapter is meant to convey its explanatory power and its claim to be essentially true. Yet it must be admitted that what we draw from this theory is insight and not practical applicability. Three phases mark its modern history. In 1931 there appeared Professor F. A. Hayek's *Prices and Production*, setting out in an almost metaphysical form the thesis that highly integrated schemes of equipment-building may overreach the society's endurance of the necessary long-sustained austerity, and thus eventually come to ruin. The relevance of such an idea for modern times needs no emphasis, the aptness of the Austrian theory of capital to formulate it and explain its mechanism seems more than ever obvious; yet the book's ascendancy, powerful though brief, was due as much to its elusiveness as to its ever-present suggestion of some powerful insight to be gained. Its readers, also its author, were impelled by this elusiveness to set about refining and re-establishing the Austrian theory of capital. They failed to exhibit the theory as a workable tool, and in especial they failed to show that the *average period of production* can be given precise meaning, let alone practical measurability. We must conclude this section by examining these difficulties.

In the foregoing we have measured the productive activity of human beings and natural forces by the 'factor-day', the work of one man on one acre of land for one day. Productive input can be measured in physical terms provided this input is homogeneous throughout all industry and all the times we are concerned with. This will be the case if there is only one factor of production, such as human labour of a given quality, or it will be the case if, when there are several factors of production, these are always combined in one and the same set of proportions no matter where or when they are at work. To make it plausible that one man should always work on one acre, neither more nor less, we have confined our discussion of the average period of production to the business of producing a single consumable commodity, and have supposed this process to be carried on in perfect isolation from that of producing any other commodity. In that discussion accordingly, the word 'average' has implied the adding together of the periods respectively elapsing between the input of each factor-day and the emergence of the attributable product, and the division of the total by the number of factor-days. Now, however, we must extend that meaning. Still maintaining the fiction that every commodity is produced in an entirely self-contained process, and that no two or more such processes have any 'intermediate products' in common, we can none the less suppose that the society has a number of such processes, and so extend our averaging of the periods elapsing between input and output to include all these various but still non-intermingling processes. Thus some further approach will be made to realism. But what now becomes of our practice of measuring input in physical terms? It is not plausible that all commodities at all stages of their manufacture should require labour and land to be combined in one and the same proportion. If the making of one commodity calls for one man on one acre and the making of another commodity calls for one man on two acres, how are we to find a meaningful 'average period' elapsing between input and output in both these two processes taken together? Only by measuring each factor in units of market value. But there is another and equally great difficulty. If the product itself comprises a number of distinct commodities, how are we to compare the results of organizing production in this way or in that? If commodity *A* is produced by applying labour and land one month before the emergence of the consumable product, while commodity *B* requires two months, then a shift of labour and land from *A* to *B* will in some degree necessarily increase the average period of production. But unless we measure output as well as factors in terms of market value, we cannot show whether or not the longer period yields a 'larger' output. In fact, in a many-product economy, there can be no measuring either of factors or of output in physical terms: we must have recourse to the great solvent, market price, which dissolves all the technically heterogeneous valuta into their homogeneous value. But this dissolving away of physical quantity reveals yet another problem, which physical measurement has enabled us hitherto to conceal. For the same reason that factors and product are to be measured by value, so must the size of the ever-existing stock of goods in process. But the value of this stock will include, not only the value at which the services of men and natural forces were reckoned when these were applied to the production of the goods which compose this stock, but also the contribution of value made by the lapse of time itself, or as we may alternatively say, made by the existence of the stock of goods itself, which allows the labour and land services to be used efficiently. Let us return, then, to the consideration of a single isolated process which yields a single consumable commodity. Each parcel of this good, as it progresses from stage to stage of manufacture, must be conceived to gain in value not only through the daily application of fresh doses of labour and land services, but by the passage of time, whose effect we can represent as a daily gain of some fixed percentage of the value at which the parcel started that day. And this presents us with the question: How is this percentage determined? What circumstances bring it to, or hold it at, some particular level?

When this question is put forward as an objection to the whole Böhm-Bawerkian scheme, the argument, expressed by means of the vehicle we have devised for that scheme, runs thus:

With any one available technology which might be chosen, the size of the capital stock, measured in value, will depend on the daily percentage at which the value of each parcel grows by the passage of time. But that percentage itself, since it reflects the extra efficiency of one technology as compared with another, and this extra efficiency, in order to be employed, requires a longer average period of production, which is to say a larger capital stock, which in turn means a lower marginal productivity of the capital stock, will depend on the size of the latter. We appear to have a circular argument in which the daily percentage rate of growth of each parcel belonging to the capital stock depends on the total size of that stock, but in which also the total size of the stock depends on the daily percentage rate of growth of the value of each parcel. If this argument were valid, it would evidently defeat Böhm-Bawerk's chief purpose, which is to show how the income derived from a capital stock of goods in process of manufacture, which income consists precisely in the daily growth, by time lapse alone, of the value of each parcel composing this stock, is determined.

But the argument is not valid. Beside each item in a list of the available technologies we could write down the average time elapsing *per value-unit of product* between the input of labour or land services, measured in value, and the emergence of their atttributable product. The members of the society would thus be given a range of clear-cut possibilities amongst which to choose. All else is needless and even harmful complication of the issue. The members of the society may evidently be expected to distribute their productive efforts over the various lines of production, that is, over the processes leading to the various consumable commodities, in such a way as to equalize the daily percentage at which the value of productive services invested in this line and that grows in value. Such distribution merely conforms to the universal rule of economy, the equalization of the marginal effects, measured by market value, of using a versatile resource for this and for that technically distinct purpose. A unique daily percentage rate of growth of value being thus supposed to be achieved, this rate will determine the income of the owners of the capital stock, since that part of the growth of value of the composing items of the stock, which is due to pure lapse of time, is the source of that income.

Let us now try to bring the whole structure and significance of the model into focus at one time. Whatever inferences we may seek to draw from the model, the thing which it explicitly describes is a stationary state, the economic affairs of a society where each day precisely reproduces the events and situations of each earlier day. We are of course free to compare a number of such societies, differing from each other in various respects, and to look upon their differences in some one respect as essentially linked with their differences in one or more other respects. Such a method is 'comparative statics'. In any one such society, however, we disregard any question of change. Thus there can be no accumulation of wealth, and however much is produced in any day, an equivalent amount must be consumed in that day. This must be true, not merely of the total value created in any day, a total value which takes the form of the progress of various parcels of goods towards completion, but it must be true of each distinct consumable commodity separately. Moreoever, since we deem each such commodity to emerge from an isolated process having no physical or mechanical connection with any other, we can study each such process by itself and merely combine them as it were 'additively' to get a picture of the whole productive effort of the society. In each such process, value is thought of as being created in two ways: first, by the input of labour-land services, and secondly by the superior efficiency in using these services achieved by technologies which require a longer average lapse of time between the application of a dose of input and its attributable output. Because the longer average lapse of time *permits* the adoption of a technology which gives a higher ratio of value of product to value of labour–land input, we can attribute the extra value of product achieved in a long as compared with a short productive process, using a *given* daily quantity of labour–land input, to the time-lapse itself, or to its material manifestation and embodiment, the stock of 'parcels' of partly-processed goods. Thus we conceive the value of each daily dose of labour–land input to increase, so long as it remains 'embodied' in a parcel of goods in process, by some constant daily percentage depending on the technology adopted. Let this percentage be s. Then if the value of each daily quantity of labour–land services applied to any one 'parcel' is u, and the total production-history of a parcel lasts T days, we have for the value of the parcel after the lapse of x days

$$(v)x = u + u(1+s) + u(1+s)^2 + \ldots + u(1+s)^x$$

$$= u \sum_{j=0}^{x} (1+s)^j.$$

Now on any and every day there will exist one parcel at each of the T distinct stages of the type of process which yields our particular commodity, and so the total value of the parcels leading to this commodity, which exist together on any one day, is

$$K = u \sum_{x=1}^{T} \sum_{j=0}^{x} (1+s)^j.$$

The output, or daily production, of the finished commodity, is the completed value of one parcel, viz.

$$Z = u \sum_{j=0}^{T} (1+s)^j,$$

of which Tu is the daily income of the suppliers of labour–land services and $Z - Tu$ is the daily income of the owners of the capital stock. This income of the capitalists is sK, since by 'lapse of time' the value of every parcel of goods composing the capital stock, and therefore the value of the capital stock itself, is augmented in a proportion s every day. The capital stock receives, each day, a *total* augmentation of $Tu + sK$ and is depleted by an equal amount as the goods completed on that day are withdrawn from the stock and consumed. All that we have been saying applies to the production and consumption of the one particular commodity.

The total model of the society's production–consumption activity represents, of course, an equilibrium or position of complete adjustment. The aggregate income derived from the production of all the consumable commodities taken together must be conceived to be used for the purchase of these commodities in a market. Each commodity will be produced in such daily quantity, by such a technology, that, given the tastes of the society, the daily percentage of value augmentation through time-lapse, s, is one and the same at all stages of all processes. This, as we said above, is merely the condition for maximization of the society's income under the constraint of its available resources, amongst which we must include, as being of the essence of the matter, its capacity and willingness to maintain a structure of production where a certain interval elapses, on the average, between input of labour–land services and the emergence of the attributable product.

In the model which we have been describing, it is possible to say unequivocally that out of the total of factor-days which went to the manufacture of some identified parcel of ready consumable goods, such-and-such a proportion was contributed on such-and-such a day, such-and-such a proportion on such-and-such another day, and so on, so that the sum and the average of the elapsed periods between input and output can be reckoned. The same reckoning can be performed the other way round, and out of the total land–labour input on any one day we can say how much serves to complete the parcel which will be consumed tomorrow, how much goes into the parcel to be consumed on the following day, and so on. There is no difficulty about the attribution of dated results to dated productive services. The same would be true under somewhat relaxed assumptions, where we supposed that the stream of input of labour–land services into any one parcel was varying instead of constant. There could still be a stationary economy keeping in being a capital stock of constant size and there could still be unequivocal linking of dated inputs and dated outputs. Our model achieves this by confining itself to the case known in the literature of Austrian capital theory as 'continuous input, point output'. Each parcel of goods, though produced by a stream of inputs during some stretch of time, is supposed to be completed and destroyed in consumption at some particular instant. It is not, that is to say, a durable tool able to render consumable or other services on a variety of different dates. Even if it were, we should still not be in a difficulty, provided we could suppose that the tool, though lasting a long time in use, was all made in an instant. This would be the point input, continuous output case. It is when we come to the realistic case of continuous input, continuous output that the attribution problem appears unsolvable. Yet we may reasonably ask how serious this problem is for a theory which claims only to give insight: the working life of a machine, still more of a building, may be a hundred times as long as the time taken to fashion it, and we could claim that the point input, continuous output case is nearly enough represented. Reality differs from the Austrian model in a more interesting respect, namely, that so far from there being an isolated, self-contained process leading up to each consumable good, there is, instead, an intricate interweaving of all the paths along which we can conceive the results of productive activity to flow through the system. We shall briefly describe in the next section the modern method of studying this interdependence of industries and its consequences. What we have sought to do above is very freely to gloss the Austrian theory of the time-structure of production, offering an account of it which may depart widely from the original in order to show that Böhm-Bawerk's and Hayek's thought is not destroyed in its essence by the criticism which has been directed at their formulations. We began this chapter, not with the Austrian model itself, but with a construction designed to show that the idea of a time-structure of production is relevant, and can be conceptually made apparent, even where there is an intricate interdependence of industries. Let us now try to bring the pure Austrian model face-to-face with those more complex conditions. The Austrian model rests essentially on the hypothesis that men would prefer to consume the fruits of their efforts in a shorter rather than a longer time from the date of those efforts. Indeed, the original version of the theory supposes that most men, possessing no reserves of consumable goods, *must* consume without delay the equivalent of what they could have produced by primitive methods requiring no stock of goods in process, no capital stock of 'intermediate products'. Thus they are willing to exchange their productive powers for that equivalent, leaving the whole excess of what can in fact be produced by advanced, capital-requiring methods, over what could have been produced by primitive methods, to the owners of the capital stock. Now there are two distinct sets of circumstances in which this 'impatience to consume' could be supposed to operate. The 'impatience' has to be overcome, in some degree and over some period, in order to build up 'from the beginning' a stock of goods suitable to some advanced technology. But when this stock is already in existence, the impatience has still to be held in check, because if it were given free rein the capital stock could be dissipated in an orgy of consumption or of indolence, of consuming more than was currently being produced. Now the question is, are these cases symmetric? Could 'building down' the capital stock proceed in an exact mirror image of building it up? May it not be true that the degree of restraint needed to preserve an existing capital stock in being is less than that needed to carry through the latest stages of advance to its present state? There are here a psychological and a technical aspect quite distinct from each other. On the one hand, the instinct to preserve may be more imperious than the ambition to advance. Only a disintegrating or a dying society, except in war, would indulge in general disinvestment. The technical question is more interesting. When the material embodiment of an advanced technology is being built up from small beginnings (in a 'take-off' unassisted by other societies) the *means* of making more advanced and specialized tools and machines and materials are themselves *less* specialized. But will it be at all profitable, even in the shortest run, to dismantle the dynamos, the telephone systems and the computers in order to use the copper of their substance for some more primitive purpose? Any widespread injury to the system as it exists and as it lives may well be fatal. The great flood of goods of rich and powerful variety will stop, to be replaced by what? We must not exaggerate. The disinvestment could conceivably be carried through with careful discrimination, leaving at each stage as much, in value terms, of the system still in working order as possible. But to what purpose? The gain in immediate consumption could at best be slight, and would last for only the briefest time. The growth and evolution of a capital-using, highly specialized economy is virtually an irreversible process. It must be profoundly doubtful whether we can really suppose that not less than some given annual percentage of the value of the capital stock must be paid to its owners as the *sine qua non* of their not beginning to disinvest it; and this will be true, no matter whether those owners are individuals or the state. Böhm-Bawerk called such income 'interest', but, as we have pointed out, he was not concerned with the idea of money in the full sense, and built a model which has no place for it. Thus the income which he called 'interest' would in Marshallian terms be called 'quasi-rent'. Society has its momentum, its 'dynamic', one aspect of which is necessarily the economic one. The full meaning and relevance of this idea have been gradually appreciated over the last thirty years. Keynes showed that in a society whose members, individually, wish to save, prosperity depends upon investment. Harrod and others have shown that investment depends for its incentive upon growth: growth of population and the desire for growth of income per head. Böhm-Bawerk's construction in terms of comparative statics leaves worlds unsaid; yet Böhm-Bawerk was a master mind.

6.3 *Leontief's input–output model*

Böhm-Bawerk's purpose was to show how it is that in a society which regulates its affairs by means of the market, and uses an advanced technology made possible by an accumulation of goods serving as instruments of production, a share of the society's total income will flow naturally to the owners of this equipment. He showed also what circumstances will govern the size of this share. To do these things he had to anatomize the business of production as a whole in a certain fashion, showing that when one instrument serves to make another in a long sequence, the consumable fruits of the work done on any day will only be reaped by society as a whole on a much later day. Thus the Austrian theory divides the whole business of producing any one consumable commodity into 'stages of production', some nearer and some more remote, in both technical sequence and in time, from the stage of ultimate sale of the commodity to a consumer. We have seen, however, that this scheme of anatomization leaves out an essential aspect of modern production, namely, that every plant and industry stands at the confluence of many streams of products which are supplied to it by other firms, and is also the point from which many streams of its own products diverge, first to other firms which it directly supplies, and through them to a great part of the whole economy. To show the important consequences of this latter aspect of the structure of production, a new scheme of anatomization was introduced during the nineteen-thirties by Wassily Leontief. In order to complete and correct, in some degree, the picture given by the Austrian theory, we shall briefly explain Leontief's basic model.

The rectangular array, composed of *m* rows and *n* columns of numbers or algebraic symbols, so arranged that each such number or symbol belongs both to a row and to a column, offers the economist a notational tool of the greatest efficiency and beauty. These two qualities are doubtless intimately linked, for notational suggestiveness, economy and flexibility can drive the vehicle of formal deductive reasoning along almost on their own. For the mathematician these arrays are the matrices and vectors whose properties and rules of manipulation constitute matrix algebra. A special case is the square array, with equal numbers of rows and of columns. It serves to express with extreme synoptic compactness the accounting identities amongst a number of firms, industries, sectors or national economies, arising from their trade with each other. A square array can serve this visual purpose independently of any manipulations, yet its analytic and interpretive power is immensely extended by application of the simplest operations of matrix algebra.

Let us suppose the society to be divided into parts which supply each other with goods. We can think of the whole world divided into nations, or of a single nation's productive activity divided into industries or into firms. Since the goods supplied by one part to another will in general be heterogeneous, we will suppose these goods all to be valued by a market, so that all the goods passing within some unit time-interval from one part of society to another can be treated as one whole and this whole measured by its value. We need a scheme for displaying at a glance the whole pattern of such transfers of goods amongst the parts of society, which occur either 'per year', etc., or within some named and identified interval such as the year 1963. The square array perfectly serves this purpose. We write the list of our *transactors*, or parts of society, twice in the self-same sequence, once as the labels of the rows of the square array and once as the labels of its columns. The value of goods passing in the specified interval from transactor *A* to transactor *B* is written in the row labelled *A* and the column labelled *B*. Thus a *single* entry shows both aspects of the transaction: how much was parted with, by whom; and by whom this amount was received. Each transactor who parts with goods of a certain value can be supposed to receive money of the same value, and each transactor who receives goods can be supposed to pay money of their value. Which aspect we elect to attend to will depend on our immediate purpose. Since each of our 'transactors' can comprise a number of individuals or firms, a transactor in our general and abstract sense can supply goods or money to itself. By sub-dividing society more finely, by distinguishing a greater number of productive 'sectors', we could eliminate all transactors who might be supposed to transfer goods to themselves, and so have a square array in which all the entries *A* to *A*, *B* to *B*, etc., would be zero. Because we take care to list our transactors always in the same sequence, these *self-to-self* entries will all lie on the *main diagonal* of our square array, running from the top left to the bottom right corner. The essence of an accounting system is coherence. For every list of items whose total (in some particular dimension, such as their market value) is shown as disposable, there must be another list whose items add up to the same total and specify what has been done with this quantity of resources. A peculiar beauty of the square array as an accounting tool is the immediacy with which this requirement is infallibly satisfied: each entry being both an item of what is parted with by the transactors all taken together, and at the same time an item of what is received by the transactors all taken together, there can be no discrepancy between the totals. We can also check at a glance whether each separate transactor's total of outgoings is equal to his total of incomings; that is to say, whether his row-total is equal to his column-total.

Input–output analysis seeks to solve the following problem: daily (etc.) supplies of a given product are in general wanted not only by those who will permanently sink these supplies in their personal sustenance and enjoyment, in the construction of durable objects or in the service of government, but also by those who will transform the substance of the given product in bringing forth further products. Let us call the former class of demand for any product *final use* and the latter class *intermediate use*. In general, every product may enter into the production of every other product, and so the total daily quantity required of any product will be a function of the daily final-use quantities required of all products. If, for all products, we are given a list of the respective daily quantities required for final use, what will be the daily quantity required of each product for both uses, intermediate and final, taken together? In order to solve such a problem numerically, the assumption is made that a fixed coefficient can be found showing how much of product A is required, as a technical minimum, in the making of a unit of product B, and that no more than this technical minimum will ever in fact be used. (Such an assumption can be justified by a variety of arguments and its practical advantages are very great.) These technical coefficients having been once observed in a particular society, their supposed constancy in that society permits us to change at will the desired 'bill of goods', that is, the list of product-quantities required for *final* use, and thence to work out for each product the total daily or yearly quantity which must be produced to satisfy both the intermediate and the final uses taken together.

Let us suppose that our society has n sectors or industries and n distinct products, and that each sector or industry produces only one product and each product is produced by only one sector or industry. We can thus use interchangeably, for many purposes, the words *sector* (or *industry*), *activity* and *product*. Let us label these sectors with numbers 1 up to n. These numbers in their natural sequence, starting from the top left-hand corner, will also label the n rows and the n columns of a square matrix or array called a transactions matrix. At each intersection of a row and column of this matrix, we can write the number expressing the total value of product supplied by the row-sector to the column sector in the relevant time-interval. The total of the entries we have thus made in any row will show how much, by value, of the product of that sector is required by other sectors for their own productive purposes; that is to say, it will show the total *intermediate use* of the product of that sector. We shall write these row-totals, one for each row (sector) in an $(n + 1)^{st}$ column at the right-hand side of the $n \times n$ transactions array. In yet a further $(n + 2)^{nd}$ column we shall show, for each sector, the value of that sector's product made available in the relevant time interval for *final use*. In an $(n + 3)^{rd}$ column we shall add together, for each row, the intermediate use and the final use of the product to get its *total use*, that is, the total quantity (by value) of that particular product which must daily emerge and be absorbed either in final use or in the production of other products. Now at the bottom of the $n \times n$ transactions array we must similarly have three further *rows*. The $(n + 1)^{st}$ row will show for each sector the column-total of *produced inputs purchased* by that sector. An $(n + 2)^{nd}$ row will show for each sector the value of its *primary inputs*, the services of labour, natural forces and such equipment as by its nature is likely to long outlast the time-interval concerned. In an $(n + 3)^{rd}$ row at the very bottom we shall show for each sector the column-total of all its inputs, both those consisting of a product supplied to it by some other sector and those consisting of primary inputs. Within the $n \times n$ array of inter sectoral transactions, each entry can be labelled by using as subscripts its row number followed by its column number, so that the general symbol for a value X passing from sector i to sector j will be X_{ij}. The production picture as a whole, with these conventions, will look like Fig. 6.1.

Listed in a column at the left-hand side are the sectors $1, 2, \ldots i, \ldots n$ in their aspect or capacity as *producers* of output which each supplies to a number of other sectors. Each sector named (numbered) in this column is the label of a row of entries each showing how much of its product (by value at constant price) the labelling sector provides for use in further transformation by each of the other sectors and perhaps by itself. In a row along the top of the table the sectors, in the same sequence as before, are listed in their aspect or capacity as *users* of each other's products. Thus the *row* in which an entry stands shows which sector *supplied* the quantity in question, the *column* in which it stands shows which sector *purchased and used* the quantity in question. Each of these transaction-quantities is represented by a symbol of the general type X_{ij}.

It will be understood that when we refer to sector i we are referring to the *representative* of all sectors in their capacity as producers. What is stated as true of sector 2 or sector 5 need not be true of sector 3 or sector 4. But what is stated as true of sector i is true of every sector.

		Purchasing sectors						Total intermediate use	Final use	Total use $Z_i = U_i + Y_i$
		1	2	---	j	---	n			
Producing sectors	1	X_{11}	X_{12}	---	X_{1j}	---	X_{1n}	W_1+	$Y_1=$	Z_1
	2	X_{21}	X_{22}	---	X_{2j}	---	X_{2n}	W_2+	$Y_2=$	Z_2
	⋮	⋮	⋮		⋮		⋮	⋮	⋮	⋮
	i	X_{i1}	X_{i2}	---	X_{ij}	---	X_{in}	W_i+	$Y_i=$	Z_i
	⋮	⋮	⋮		⋮		⋮	⋮	⋮	⋮
	n	X_{n1}	X_{n2}	---	X_{nj}	---	X_{nn}	W_n+	$Y_n=$	Z_n
Total produced inputs		U_1	U_2		U_j		U_n	$U \equiv W$		
Primary inputs		V_1	V_2		V_j		V_n		$V \equiv Y$	
Total production		Z_1	Z_2		Z_j		Z_n			Z

Fig. 6.1

The row-total of sector i is represented by the symbol W_i. The column-total of sector j is represented by the symbol U_j. The *total of the row-totals*, that is, the total value of all products supplied by the sectors to each other in the given time-interval, may be written $\sum_{i=1}^{n} W_i$ or simply W without subscript. Similarly the *total of the column totals* is

$$\sum_{j=1}^{n} U_j = U$$

representing the total value of all products received by the sectors from each other. Plainly by their meaning $U \equiv W$. We may notice that there is no reason in general for U_i to be equal to W_i. If, by chance, it happened that sector i had the same total of intermediate use of its own product as of purchases from other sectors, this would be a casual or circumstantial equality, and we should write it with the two-barred symbol $U_i = W_i$. Identical equalities, however, are highly characteristic of the accounting idea in general and of the input–output model in particular, and we find several important instances in Fig. 6.1. First, the total value of *primary inputs* to all sectors taken together is necessarily equal to the *value added* by productive activity as a whole, and also to the total value of goods made available for *final use* by all sectors taken together. These identities are easy to appreciate intuitively. In the input–output model, inter-sectoral transfers of value are not conceived as themselves creating any value. Value goes into the productive machine as a whole from outside, in the form of primary, non-produced inputs of labour and natural forces and the services of durable equipment, and comes out from it in the form of goods available for final use, that is, for consumption, the creation of extra durable equipment, and the purposes of government. What goes on inside the mixing-bowl is, indeed, our object of study, but only the equivalent of the ingredients which are put into it comes out of it. A second identical equality is that of the total purchases of produced inputs by all sectors taken together to the total of goods for intermediate use supplied by all sectors taken together:

$$\sum_{j=1}^{n} U_j \equiv \sum_{i=1}^{n} W_i.$$

This illustrates what we have called in Chapter IV an identical equality of type *A*, it is a case of one thing seen from two viewpoints. Finally, it is evident that total production is one and the same whether we reckon it as the total value, in all sectors taken together, of produced and non-produced inputs:

$$\sum_{j=1}^{n} U_j + \sum_{j=1}^{n} V_j \equiv \sum_{j=1}^{n} Z_j \equiv Z,$$

or whether we reckon it as the total value, in all sectors together, of goods supplied for intermediate use and of goods made available for final use:

$$\sum_{i=1}^{n} W_i + \sum_{i=1}^{n} Y_i \equiv \sum_{i=1}^{n} Z_i \equiv Z.$$

What Fig. 6.1 provides is a system of pigeon-holes. We come now to the sequence of operations, and of links in the chain of thought, by which this scheme is used to answer the questions: What set of total outputs of the n products will be needed to provide a *given and pre-selected* set of daily (annual, etc.) quantities available for final use? And what, therefore, must be the quantities of primary inputs into each sector?

The first stage is to fill in the pigeon-holes with numerical values derived from statistics of the state of our society at some one time. The second stage is to work out the input coefficients by dividing each purchased quantity of product k, or of primary input l, used in the making of product p, by the total quantity produced of product p. We thus replace the n columns of absolute quantities (measured by value at constant prices) of goods purchased by one sector from another, by n columns of the ratios of these quantities to the total production, for both intermediate and final use taken together, of each of the products. At the bottom of each of these new columns (which taken together make up an $n \times n$ matrix) we have in addition the input coefficient of primary input, got by dividing the quantity of primary input required by each product by the total quantity produced of that product. The result is shown in Fig. 6.2.

Each entry of Fig. 6.2 is a division sum showing dividend, divisor and quotient, the latter being represented by a symbol of the form a_{ij} and showing how much of the product of sector i must be used as input into sector j to make possible the production of a unit of product j. Fig. 6.2 is thus a *matrix of input coefficients* and can be written in less cluttered form as in Fig. 6.3.

Let us consider the meaning of this array of coefficients. If we take them one row at a time, and multiply the first element (coefficient) in this row by the total production in sector 1, then multiply the second element of the row by the total production in sector 2, and, in general, the jth element of the row by the total production in sector j, and having worked thus through the whole row, we then add together the resulting answers of these multiplications, we get the total *intermediate use* of product 1. Doing the same for the second row of coefficients, we get the total intermediate use of product 2; and so on. And

Purchasing sectors

		1	2	---	j	---	n
Producing sectors	1	$\frac{X_{11}}{Z_1} = a_{11}$	$\frac{X_{12}}{Z_2} = a_{12}$	---	$\frac{X_{1j}}{Z_j} = a_{1j}$	---	$\frac{X_{1n}}{Z_n} = a_{1n}$
	2	$\frac{X_{21}}{Z_1} = a_{21}$	$\frac{X_{22}}{Z_2} = a_{22}$	---	$\frac{X_{2j}}{Z_j} = a_{2j}$	---	$\frac{X_{2n}}{Z_n} = a_{2n}$
	⋮	⋮	⋮		⋮		⋮
	i	$\frac{X_{i1}}{Z_1} = a_{i1}$	$\frac{X_{i2}}{Z_2} = a_{i2}$	---	$\frac{X_{ij}}{Z_j} = a_{ij}$	---	$\frac{X_{in}}{Z_n} = a_{in}$
	⋮	⋮	⋮		⋮		⋮
	n	$\frac{X_{n1}}{Z_1} = a_{n1}$	$\frac{X_{n2}}{Z_2} = a_{n2}$	---	$\frac{X_{nj}}{Z_j} = a_{nj}$	---	$\frac{X_{nn}}{Z_n} = a_{nn}$
Primary input value added per unit of total production		$\frac{V_1}{Z_1}$	$\frac{V_2}{Z_2}$		$\frac{V_j}{Z_j}$		$\frac{V_n}{Z_n}$

Fig. 6.2

$$\begin{bmatrix} a_{11} & a_{12} & \cdot & \cdot & \cdot & a_{1j} & \cdot & \cdot & \cdot & a_{1n} \\ a_{21} & a_{22} & \cdot & \cdot & \cdot & a_{2j} & \cdot & \cdot & \cdot & a_{2n} \\ \cdot & \cdot & & & & \cdot & & & & \cdot \\ \cdot & \cdot & & & & \cdot & & & & \cdot \\ \cdot & \cdot & & & & \cdot & & & & \cdot \\ a_{i1} & a_{i2} & \cdot & \cdot & \cdot & a_{ij} & \cdot & \cdot & \cdot & a_{in} \\ \cdot & \cdot & & & & \cdot & & & & \cdot \\ \cdot & \cdot & & & & \cdot & & & & \cdot \\ \cdot & \cdot & & & & \cdot & & & & \cdot \\ a_{n1} & a_{n2} & \cdot & \cdot & \cdot & a_{nj} & \cdot & \cdot & \cdot & a_{nn} \end{bmatrix}$$

Fig. 6.3

if, for each product 1, 2, . . . i, . . . n in turn, we subtract the total intermediate use from the total production, what is left is the (daily or annual, etc.) quantity available for final use. Thus we have for product i

$$Z_i - \sum_{j=1}^{n} a_{ij} Z_j = Y_i.$$

What would be desirable is a shorthand notation indicating that the series of operations whose result is thus summed up should be performed, as we have described above, for each product in turn, and such a notation is provided by the rule of multiplication of matrices and vectors which is a central convention of matrix algebra. This rule provides that if an $n \times m$ matrix stands to the left of an $m \times l$ matrix, the two matrices can be multiplied together, and that this is to be done in the following way. Imagine the first column of the right-hand matrix to be bodily lifted and superposed on the first row of the left-hand matrix, the elements thus paired being multiplied together and the results of these multiplications added. The possibility of such pairing is ensured by our stipulation that the two matrices are $n \times m$ and $m \times l$, so that the left-hand one has as many elements in a row as the right-hand one has elements in a column. We next move the column which we lifted from the right-hand matrix and superpose it on the second row of the left-hand matrix, multiply the paired elements and add the answers; and so on for all the rows of the left-hand matrix. The result is a column of numbers which constitute the first column of the $n \times l$ matrix which we shall obtain by the total business of multiplying together the two original matrices. The *second* column of this final matrix is got by using the *second* column of the right-hand multiplicand matrix, and so on Thus for example:

$$\begin{bmatrix} a_{11} & a_{12} & a_{13} \\ a_{21} & a_{22} & a_{23} \\ a_{31} & a_{32} & a_{33} \end{bmatrix} \begin{bmatrix} Z_1 \\ Z_2 \\ Z_3 \end{bmatrix} = \begin{bmatrix} a_{11}Z_1 + a_{12}Z_2 + a_{13}Z_3 \\ a_{21}Z_1 + a_{22}Z_2 + a_{23}Z_3 \\ a_{31}Z_1 + a_{32}Z_2 + a_{33}Z_3 \end{bmatrix}$$

is the 3×1 matrix obtained by multiplying together a 3×3 and a 3×1 matrix, the former standing *on the left* of the latter. (It would be impossible to multiply a 3×1 matrix by a 3×3

matrix standing on its *right*, for the number of elements in a row of the former would not be the same as the number of elements in a column of the latter.)

It can be seen at once that if the left-hand of the foregoing matrices, which we can write for short (a_{ij}) or simply capital A is the matrix of input coefficients in a 3-sector economy, while the left-hand matrix (Z_j), or simple Z is the vector of total quantities respectively produced in these sectors, the 3-element vector AZ which results from multiplying them together gives the total intermediate use quantities for all three sectors. Thus we can re-write the equation of p. 179 above in an alternative form. Instead of

$$Z_i - \sum_{j=1}^{n} a_{ij} Z_j = Y_i$$

we shall have, if $n = 3$,

$$Z - AZ = Y,$$

where Y is the 3-element vector of quantities (of the three products) available for final use. Just as in elementary algebra $z - az = y$ could be re-written $(1 - a)z = y$, so we can introduce a matrix which plays a similar part in matrix algebra to that of the number 1 in ordinary algebra, namely to *leave unchanged* anything multiplied by it. The $n \times n$ *identity matrix*, written I, is

$$I = \begin{bmatrix} 1 & 0 & 0 & . & . & . & . & 0 \\ 0 & 1 & 0 & . & . & . & . & 0 \\ . & . & . & . & . & . & . & . \\ . & . & . & . & . & . & . & . \\ . & . & . & . & . & . & . & . \\ . & . & . & . & . & . & . & . \\ 0 & 0 & 0 & . & . & . & . & 1 \end{bmatrix}$$

and the 3×3 identity matrix is

$$I = \begin{bmatrix} 1 & 0 & 0 \\ 0 & 1 & 0 \\ 0 & 0 & 1 \end{bmatrix}.$$

Thus finally, our equation will read

$$(I - A)Z = Y.$$

The matrix $I - A$, which in our 3-sector economy will be

$$I - A = \begin{bmatrix} 1 - a_{11} & - a_{12} & - a_{13} \\ - a_{21} & 1 - a_{22} & - a_{23} \\ - a_{31} & - a_{32} & 1 - a_{33} \end{bmatrix}$$

is called the Leontief matrix. It illustrates the rule for addition or subtraction of one matrix from another, which can only be done when both of them are $n \times m$ matrices, and consists in adding together corresponding elements (elements belonging to the same row and the same column in the respective matrices) or subtracting them one from another.

One more step. What we wish to find out is the vector Z (the list) of the total quantities which must be produced, one quantity for each product, for both intermediate and final use taken together, if we are to have a given, or freely chosen, vector Y of quantities available for *final* use. When, in ordinary algebra, we wish to find the value of x in terms of the constants a and b in the equation $ax = b$, we multiply both sides of the equation by the reciprocal of a, viz. a quantity which, when multiplied by a gives unity, and so we get $x = \frac{b}{a}$. In matrix algebra the *inverse* of a square matrix M is defined as that matrix M^{-1} which, when multiplied by M, gives the identity matrix I: $MM^{-1} = I$. Now suppose we can find a matrix R such that $R(I - A) = I$. Then multiplying by it both sides of our matrix equation

$$(I - A)Z = Y,$$

we have
$$R(I - A)Z = RY$$

or
$$Z = RY.$$

Performing the multiplications of appropriately paired elements indicated by RY, we get the column-vector or list, Z, of total quantities to be produced in the respective sectors. Such is the kind of result aimed at by input–output analysis.

More than most branches of knowledge, economics is an artificial subject. It does not seek to understand the whole human being, intellect and feelings, instinctual knowledge or race-memories, curiosity, imagination and all that that embraces and implies. It by no means concerns itself even with the whole of social action and organization. It deals only with the market-oriented part of life. Thus in economics there cannot be that ultimate *simplicity of Nature*, in faith of which, natural scientists strive to unify physics, chemistry and biology, and, in their more visionary moments, to find the single principle of things. Economics, like every discipline because of the very nature of *systematic* knowledge, must impose a simplicity on its subject-matter. But if this simplicity cannot be discovered at the heart of things, it must instead be constructed, its lines must be in large degree arbitrary. Let us admit that all science is 'arbitrary'. As we sit before the fire, we see patterns and pictures in the flames. These patterns can be selected in an infinity of infinities of different ways. Just so can those stereotypes of concomitant or sequential circumstances, which we call cause and effect or natural law, be discovered in countless ways; for ultimately these patterns depend on, are composed of, and bind together, concepts which are thought-constructs of our own. But unquestionably Nature offers powerful suggestions. The imagination of the natural scientist is nudged and prompted by the never-ceasing stream of almost exactly repetitive and almost self-classifying events. The scientist of human affairs has had in much greater measure to be a romantic, a maker of fictions. Because his material of study is more superficial, more the end-product of an unthinkably complex and subtle interplay of the elements of human character and situation, he has had to invent frames of reference and schemes of classification which are much less easily referable to 'fact' than those of the natural scientist.

For these reasons the seeker of a theory of human affairs, and especially of economic affairs, can justly claim a certain licence. The student of Leontief's input–output analysis may reasonably ask just what is the basis or *apologia* for assuming fixed ratios of purchased materials to output of an industry. Are these coefficients fixed by technical necessity? Are they the expression of a statistical stability resulting from the aggregation of a wide diversity of individual technical or psychological phenomena each quite variable in itself? Let us then make this claim. The great economists have been the great simplifiers. But in economics, simplification is an arbitrary and an inevitably *drastic* act. The powerful theories, effective in cutting through the tangle of phenomena and providing a vista, a line of thought, are inevitably ruthless. The ultimate test of a theory is perhaps the pragmatic one: does it lead to successful action? But that test may be long in declaring itself. Meanwhile there is another test: the aesthetic. Beauty may reasonably be sought in theories as in other works, and applauded when it is found.

CHAPTER VII

A SCHEME OF ECONOMIC THEORY

Time in some sort, or else the absence of time in any sort, is essential to the nature and meaning of each of the models we have discussed. Let us consider their differences in respect of such time-involvement. Equilibrium means for us a set of actions, bi-uniquely corresponding to a set of individuals, each of which actions is chosen by some individual out of a range of actions available to him, in perfect and complete knowledge of what other actions are going to compose the set and in complete disregard of all actions not belonging to the set. In this conception, temporal sequence of earlier and later, 'duration' or cumulation of effect, time-extension, past and future, have no meaning, and we may call this model timeless. In contrast, a model of systematic movement is a list of classes of measurements, each class defined by its subject-matter and not by its date, and for each such class of measurements, an equation showing how the particular measurement representing that class on a particular date is to be calculated from the particular measurements representing other classes on the same *or other* dates, consistency being of course assumed amongst the equations of the model. The time-idea essential to such a model is that of a *distancing* from each other of the dates of some of those measurements which are linked by the equations. The model need be in no way concerned with the identification of its dates by reference to episodes of some history external to it. On the contrary, it is entirely self-contained. Thus we may call it non-historical. We are to think of a calendar-axis scaled in unit intervals from some arbitrary zero point, and of another, and variable, point whose increasing rightward distance from this origin represents the movement of the 'present moment'. At each position of this 'present moment' any given subject-matter will yield some particular measurement, and the difference between two such measurements of a given subject-matter is an event occurring in the interval between the positions, i.e. the dates, of the two measurements. At a variety of distances to the left of the present moment, each such distance being invariant against movements of the present moment, will be found the dates of those classes of measurements on which the 'present' measurement of the subject-matter that we happen to be interested in is deemed to depend. Thus a train of variable points, rigidly distanced from each other by lesser or greater time-lags, is deemed to move bodily along the calendar axis, each being looked on as the vehicle of a different subject-matter whose measurement varies with the change of its date. It is plain that no one *subject-matter* can be picked out as 'effect' while the others are regarded as 'causes'. At most we can regard the events occurring in some subject-matters between two fixed calendar positions as part of the 'cause' of an event in another subject-matter between a more rightward pair of positions; but *every* measurement or movement of each subject-matter is both 'effect' of events to the left of it and 'cause' of events to the right of it. 'Cause and effect' badly expresses the meaning of the model, which is that of *structure involving relations of earlier and later.*

In this statement of what we mean by *model of systematic movement* we have given the words 'present moment' an extremely attentuated and denatured meaning. That variable, i.e. class of measurements, which at any stage of our argument we are looking on as the dependent variable of some equation is thought of as occupying the model's 'present moment'. An *event* occurs in such a model when this 'present moment', and all the other moving points which it trails behind it on the calendar-axis at fixed time-distances or time-lags, moves through some segment of the calendar-axis towards the right, each such point through its own immediate segment. Thus there is a sense in which, in such a model, rightwards is futurewards and leftwards is pastwards. Except in this sense, the model allows no meaning to 'past' and 'future'. Given a complete set of mutually associated numerical values of the variables, we can *calculate* not only what will happen but what has happened, as far forward or back as we like. The model is an abstract representation of perfect determinism. Nearly at the polar extreme from such a position is Keynes's conception of the unpredictable caprice of things.

Keynes's work has no place for any visible, explicit and

precise determination of the present by the past. The present has a legacy from the past, in the form of a given assemblage of equipment in the broadest sense, and a given assemblage of people with various skills and tastes and various shares in the total property of the society. Above all, however, these people have *expectations* whose fragmentary basis of news shifts and dissolves from hour to hour and allows their calculations only the most ephemeral validity. It is the variously imagined and enigmatic future which governs the 'present' momentary equilibrium. That equilibrium is brought about not only by actions but largely also by *valuations*. The value that a man sets on something, when that value is based on his notions of the present or future valuations which will be set on it by others, can change in a moment by any amount. This is the essence of the Keynesian vision and its difference from the kind of equilibrium envisaged by the Robertsonians who treated bonds and shares, those mere hostages of fortune, as though they were butter or petroleum produced, exchanged and used up day by day for the sake of their known and 'tangible' virtues. The dependence of a momentarily stable bond price on the existence of two camps of dealers, the Bulls and the Bears with their opposite assumptions about imminent price change, the instantaneous mobility from one camp to the other of unlimited proportions of the market, the swift rise or fall of price which can occur without any substantial dealings, all this was alien and unassimilable by those who thought of a market as governed by flows of production and consumption of things desired for their own sake. Keynes's model shows the character imposed on economic life by a consciousness of unknown events to come.* Those events, however dimly apprehended and however elaborately shrugged off, being things imagined have as part of their nature an imagined time, the time implicit in expectation.

* Concerning the foregoing paragraph, Professor Carter writes: 'Would it be fair to suggest that Keynes was over-impressed by the Stock Exchange, just as the Robertsonians were over-impressed by an imaginary commodity-market?' One characteristic, for which the central and basic conception to be found in the *General Theory* has not, so far as my readmg goes, been praised at all as it deserves, is its unity, its binding together of a few ideas into an indivisible structure. Thus we cannot really defend Keynes against Professor Carter's suggestion, by saying that the volatility which Keynes insisted on as a chief characteristic of expectations

Since the imagination of such events may place them in sequence, expectation-time must evidently be in some sense extensive, so as to allow for the idea that events each requiring a moment of time for its enactment occur one after the other. But that time which the detached observer or scientist constructs to provide a theatre for his models of systematic movement is also extensive. What is the need to distinguish these two conceptions of time? It arises from what is done with them. Expectational time is an aspect of a decision-maker's effort to choose a course of action in face of uncertainty about the outcome which would flow from this course or that. Mechanical time is the locus of a precise and complete structure composed from without by the detached observer. Our first distinction, providing the labels of two of the axes along which we shall order our various models, is therefore between mechanical time and expectational time, or perhaps better, between time of mechanism and time of uncertainty.

Marshall shows us the need for still a third idea of time. For Marshall set himself no less a task than the provision of a theory of economic evolution. Whether *evolution*, irreversible, non-repetitive change, can in logic lend itself to analysis is open to doubt. Science depends upon regularities, upon repetitions of path, structure or association, and evolution in its

was relevant chiefly to their role in his theory of interest. For his theory of interest was centred on the notion of liquidity preference, and liquidity is preferred when the prospects for assets other than money, and the implied impending price-movements of those other assets, seem adverse. Amongst these other assets are tools and equipment which might be ordered to be *newly produced*, and thus a preference for liquidity implies an unwillingness to perform, in large enough quantity per time-unit, that activity of net investment, that employment of resources in creating additions and improvements of the society's productive equipment, on which activity the filling of a full-employment 'saving gap' between income and consumption depends. 'Liquidity preference' is not only the reason for the existence of a positive interest-rate, it is also an expression of a (temporary) aversion from investment. Keynes may have overstressed in some degree the vulnerability of investment plans to that sort of events which occasionally cause Stock Exchange prices to plunge downwards. And yet, if these prices go low enough, surely companies with large reserves of money, or large borrowing power, can more profitably spend their money on buying up other companies than on paying for new construction? And if so, what guarantee is there that the recipients of this money, a great crowd of individual shareholders, will be swiftly organized by someone into a new investment-requiring venture through which they can put their funds back into circulation?

Keynes may have been too Stock Exchange minded. But this does nothing to rehabilitate the Robertsonian view of interest.

long-range *effects* is the negation of repetitive phenomena. If there can be a theory of evolution of any subject-matter, whether biological or social, it must lie in *mechanism*, in the basic principle which allows or directs an exploratory development. In biology such a mechanism is represented by the heritability of random mutations and the survival of those mutants and their offspring whose mutations give them an advantage in some available environment. What parallel is there to this amongst societies and their component institutions or bodies? Marshall shows how firms which achieve some increase in size are likely thereby to become more economical in production and thus to gain a competitive advantage leading to further growth. The sources of these economies of large scale are studied in detail, and the whole process of increase of scale, increase of knowledge, cheapening of price and widening of the market is exhibited as an organic unity. Marshall shows us society inevitably urging itself on, not necessarily on paths which anyone can foresee but making what Marshall in his Victorian optimism deemed to be progress. Marshall studied a segment of real history, though he studied its texture rather than its broad outline. We thus need *evolutionary time.*

Marshall's models are dynamic in a quite other sense than those of Harrod and Hicks, or those of Keynes. For Marshall's object of study was not a single spotlighted moment typical of all moments that the model can encompass, as in Harrod, nor a repetitive cycle of events as in Hicks, nor the transient coherence of a situation poised upon uncertainties, as in Keynes. It was a unique and identified episode, destined only to happen once, the progress of industrial methods and organization in late Victorian England as reflected in the prices of goods and the conditions of life of those who produced them. Marshall studied the real life of his own day and sought to reduce its essential economic forces to an intelligible abstract scheme, the long-period supply curve. We have seen how this differs from the mere representation of price as a function of output only, in a given set of other circumstances. Marshall here conceived his firm or industry, not as simply being confronted in the particular circumstances of one real-historic date with the need to select an output, and therefore a price, from a range of possibilities, but as actually *living out* its long-period supply-curve. The price-output pairings of that curve were not always (Marshall used the curve in various ways) rival possibilities but sometimes they were a chain of successive positions taken up by the firm or industry in the course of its evolution. This complex conception is the vehicle of *Marshallian evolutionary time*.

In various degrees and senses the three concepts falling under the heading *time*, that we have distinguished in this chapter, are all of them constructs, they are the *results* of thinking and not an essential condition of there being any thought. In using any of these three ideas to build our theories, we are conceiving of the individuals with whom we people those theories as themselves constructing or conceiving these notions of time. But there is a quite different class of time-notions, a class with only one member, the solitary moment of actual experience, the all-embracing present, the time *in* which the individual feels, thinks, decides and acts, and *in* which he has the *thought* which we have called mechanical, evolutionary and expectational time. One may remember the past, but this remembering is done in the present. One may imagine a future, many rival conceptions of the future, but this imagining is done in the present. *Present* thoughts and acts, so far as our consciousness can tell us, are all that *is*. To be is to be in the present.*

This time of actuality, the solitary present or moment in being, must be somehow represented in any theory of action. There is a time *at* which any given action occurs. Thus whether or not time in other senses appears in this theory or that, we cannot effectively classify theories according to their use or non-use, or even their emphasizing or not emphasizing, of a notion of *present action*. The classification or ordering must rest upon their use of other time-concepts in explaining the nature, source or determinants of action. If there are three sorts of constructed time to consider, we need a three-fold ordering of theories.

If we have grounds and tests for ordering theories according to the degrees of their dependence on some one time-construct,

* Let me say as strongly as words can that there is here intended not the least denial of transcendental realities. It is plain that what we apprehend as 'reality' is only 'the shadows cast from without into the mouth of the cave'. But it is only with these shadows that science can be concerned.

we may go further than the mere ordering of those theories which we have examined, and ask whether, when these latter have been set in sequence, there may not be cases where two adjacent theories differ considerably enough for other, perhaps not-yet-existent and merely notional theories, to be interposed between them. The question whether such interposition is in any particular case conceivable can be answered by discovering

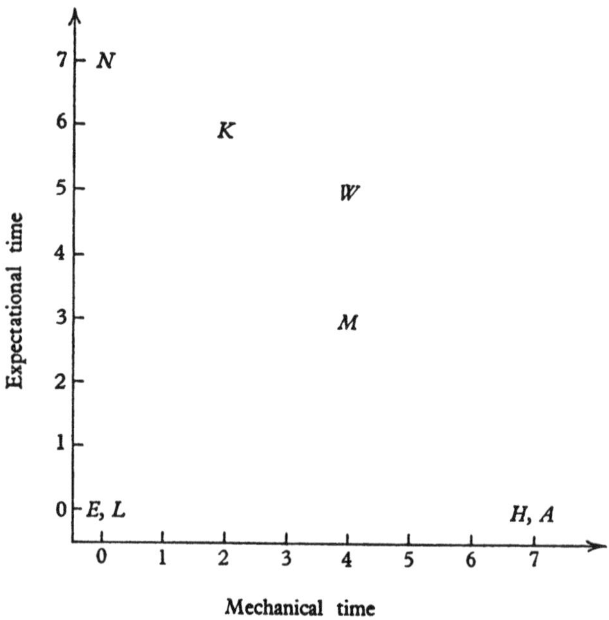

Fig. 7.1

some existing theory or inventing a new one which fits the place, or by showing in detail that such a place exists. We shall not attempt either of these methods but shall rely upon an intuitive judgement which, of course, the reader is free to replace by judgements or arguments of his own. We shall be even a little more arbitrary still, and on each axis of Fig. 7.1 we shall distinguish eight locations labelled from 0 up to 7. To assign any theory to place seven means that its involvement with time in the sense with which that ordering is concerned is central to its meaning. Place zero means of course that time is deemed to have no role in that theory.

Let us assign to each type of theory three numbers, the first locating it with respect to mechanical time, the second to evolutionary time and the third to expectational time. We wish to order in this way eight types of theory: six which we have treated explicitly, one, which we will call Neo-Wicksellian sequence analysis, which we have illustrated in our discussion of the Kahn multiplier as a process, and one, representing a pure concern with expectational time, for an account of which I must refer the reader to other books of mine.* The result is Table 7.1.

TABLE 7.1

E	General timeless equilibrium	(0,0,0)
L	Leontief models	(0,0,0)
H	Harrod–Hicks models of systematic movement	(7,0,0)
A	Austrian capital theory	(7,0,0)
M	Marshall's time-spectrum	(4,7,3)
W	Neo-Wicksellian sequence analysis	(4,0,5)
K	Keynesian kaleido-statics	(2,0,6)
N	Non-distributive expectation	(0,0,7)

The timelessness of equilibrium in our sense has been sufficiently explained, and we need scarcely justify further the assignment to it of (0, 0, 0). Leontief's model in itself is rather an instantaneous picture of a stationary process than an account of change, though one of its uses lies in the comparison of several such pictures, one for each of a number of different processes. Leontief's model can indeed serve as the basis of 'dynamic programming', the stage-by-stage prescription of how advance is to be achieved. But this is another matter. A time-structure, as well as a structure of technical interdependence (indeed the two are inseparable) is implicit in the Leontief analysis, but it is not the purpose of the model to insist upon the time-aspects of inter-industry dependence. Thus we assign it (0, 0, 0). Models of systematic movement are concerned with mechanical time alone. In Hicks's account of his model there is, very properly, almost no reference to expectation, there is certainly in this model an essential exclusion of uncertainty, indeed, an exclusion of thought and of non-empty

* *Time in Economics* (North Holland Publishing Company for the Professor F. de Vries Foundation, 1958); *Decision Order and Time in Human Affairs* (Cambridge University Press, 1961).

decision on the part of any human individual, and of any non-mechanical attributes. Thus we assign it (7, 0, 0). The Austrian theory of capital is in an important sense an account of stationary states, and a means of comparing them. But it is also intimately concerned with a process requiring lapse of time. This process is in our sense 'mechanical' although the incentive to shift from one time-structure of production to another is a response to price and profit comparisons. This type of theory seems to fit best into (7, 0, 0), since it is scarcely concerned with evolutionary time and not at all with uncertain expectation.

It is more difficult to justify a particular placing of Marshall. The aims of his long labour were peculiarly his own, a fusing of fact and theory, a conscription of the concrete and particular into service of the abstract and general. Of all his discoveries, that of the significance of time available for response, the short and long period, is perhaps the most striking. His is the only *theory* which gives pride of place to evolutionary time. Yet he is also concerned with patterns of virtually necessitated response and reaction to the circumstances arising from the earlier conduct of others, he shows how firms and industries will evolve by stages under the pressure of a shifted demand-curve. Mechanical time has a place in his account. Moreover, his wording never long leaves it in doubt that the business man is moved to do this or that by his expectations. In assigning Marshall to (4, 7, 3) we are regarding his time-spectrum of long and short periods as an aspect largely of evolutionary time. This set of numbers also calls attention to the roundedness and balance of Marshall's work; he was no intensive specialist or theoro-technician but a social philosopher.

Knut Wicksell has described a mechanism of change of the general price level by assuming (with high realism) that time elapses between the borrowing of funds for productive purposes and the sale of the resulting goods, so that the interest-rate charged by the banks for these funds can turn out to have been too low and lead to a competitive bidding up of prices of the means and results of production. The argument was formalized for the sake of clarity by supposing that all contracts were made simultaneously at intervals of a year. Wicksell's followers, in particular Erik Lindahl and Gunnar Myrdal, made the scheme into a tool of very general application, whereby the out-turn, in any chosen respect, of a just-elapsed interval is compared with the expectations held at the beginning of that interval (expectations on which the action, and thus partly the out-turn, of the interval depended) and new decisions for action in the coming interval are based on this comparison. This scheme was the first to make expectations an explicit, formal and entirely essential part of a mechanism of economic events. It thus qualifies for a rather high placing in both the expectational and the mechanistic ordering. Yet there is a dilemma. So long as it claims to show determinate results of a *mechanism* it cannot involve true uncertainty, and this statement holds in spite of the admirable elaboration of the Lindahlian–Myrdalian scheme by Dr Karl-Olof Faxén who replaced single-valued expectations held with (subjective) certainty by probability-distributions supposed to be known with certainty. For the Faxenian scheme is still determinate.

Keynes's model states the consequences of the *conventional* modes of coping with a world of ineradicable uncertainty: the assumption, *faute de mieux*, that the present look of things is a trustworthy guide to the future; the basing of business calculations on a set of data which are inevitably fragmentary and therefore exposed to radical re-interpretation with the advent of fresh news; the readiness to retreat to liquidity as soon as the business outlook becomes too obscure even in the synthetic boardroom light; the dependence of the interest-rate on the balance of forces between camps holding two opposite opinions on the direction of its next change. In Keynes's model, expectations have taken charge, and they are above the law; no attempt is made to formalize either their origin or the methods of reducing their swirling dark disorder to a basis of action. Their central role in the Keynesian conception implies for the latter a place far out in the 'expectational' ordering, but not the extreme place, for Keynes is concerned with the effects of a psychic process which he leaves unanalysed. Moreover, although the formal frame is that of the seeking of equilibrium, there are passages, such as Chapter 22 on the trade cycle, where Keynes sketches a mechanism of time-lagged reactions. To suggest all this we have placed the Keynesian model at (2, 0, 6).

The question what is *decision* itself; how a science which seeks to explain all human deliberative conduct in terms of an interaction of tastes and circumstances can concede to the word decision any substantial meaning; how there can be any room for *improvisation*, the composing, as distinct from the mere enactment, of history; the question of the nature of expectation, its sources and its mode of engendering decisions; these are the matters which should occupy a theory claiming the most extreme place on the axis of concern with expectational time. The outline of such a theory has been elsewhere attempted by the present writer.*

Models of individual and social economic action will continue to be proposed; in the nature of things there can be no foreknowledge of them. The list we have offered of types of economic model or theory is meant to schematize economic theory, in respect of its involvement of time-concepts, as it has emerged in the century since Walras's analysis of general interdependence. In offering a new reason for conceiving of an *equilibrium*, namely the need to show how action could in principle be strictly rational or how, in practice, it can approximate to rationality, we have sought also to suggest what ought to be a central strand in all economic problems and explanations, namely, the question of what knowledge *or knowledge-substitutes* can be possessed by those who choose one action out of many available. This basic question of what can be known by whose who act, and what can be done to make up for knowledge which is absent by circumstance or by the nature of things, has been much neglected by economists, despite brilliant essays by F. A. von Hayek† and Professor L. M. Lachmann.‡ At the risk of over-burdening a scheme of thought which some readers may already deem naïve, we shall conclude by trying to learn something by plotting on one diagram two of the three orderings of Table 7.1, those with respect to mechanical and expectational time. Since evolutionary time scarcely appears in any model except Marshall's, we need not compare the ordering in this respect with the other two.

The most obvious feature of Fig. 7.1 is the emptiness of the

* Needless to say, the ordering of theories according to their degree of involvement in this or that conception of time has nothing whatever to do with any question of the value or power of such theories.

† See *Economica*, New Series, Vol. IV, no. 13, February 1937

‡ See *Metroeconomica*, xi, 1959.

top right-hand corner. Is this a mere accident, a gap waiting to be filled by economic theorists or left unfilled by our own neglect of some appropriate existing work, or is it something more significant? Is this empty space one which can be filled? If expectation means, as it does in the Neo-Wicksellian models even when they employ probabilities instead of single-valued anticipations held with certainty, the determinate interpretation of, and response to, such data as may be available and also the determinateness of these data, then we are in effect back with mechanical time.* A model of type *N*, if any such can be devised acceptably, purports to show some structural aspects of an inventive thought-process, a thought-process, that is, such that it would be a contradiction in terms to claim to know what will be invented. Probability operates with the indispensable supposition that the action-chooser has for each course of action a list *known to be complete* of possible outcomes of that action. Inventive expectation implies that no such list can in logic be available to the decision-maker. The top right-hand corner of Fig. 7.1 is empty by logic and not by accident.

There is one implication which, though perhaps intuitively plain enough, is made explicit and, we think, unavoidable by such a study as we have attempted in this book, namely, the vanity of the hope of ever building, in economic terms alone, a super-model embracing the essentials of all the types we have arrayed. If models of all the types we have dissected are necessary or useful (and we think they are) we have to be content to use them one at a time, each as a means of one kind of insight into the whole phenomenon of a society in its economic behaviour. These models perform a kind of surgery, but only one part of the organism can be exposed at a time. Each model can be 'general' in some one sense or other, but not in an absolute sense. The proof of this, so far as our list of models is concerned, lies in the simple fact that they require mutually incompatible interpretations of the word 'time'. Does this condemn the whole exercise of model-building and bring us back to the position of believing only in descriptive historiography? We think not. There can be no *logical* combining of

* See the present writer's review of *Monetary and Fiscal Policy under Uncertainty*, by Karl Olof Faxén (Stockholm: Almquist and Wicksell, 1957) in the *Economic Journal*, lxix, 1959.

models; but within the mind of the social philosopher there can be a non-logical blending of the light which these models throw.

The theories or types of theory we have been examining can be classified in another way. Whether we suppose that men's conduct is pure passive response to circumstances passively conceived, or whether we suppose them capable of thoughts undetermined and unimplied by what has gone before, still the effects they can achieve are conditioned and restricted by natural laws. Or let us say: in a world containing men there may or may not be laws determining what *will* happen, laws of necessity; but there are at any rate laws which effectively limit what is *possible*. What has been called the 'pure logic of choice' is simply the definition of those ultimate constraints under which we live, constraints imposed by limited human capacity for attention, experience and exertion, by the span of natural life, and by the presence of rival humans in our world of limited space and limited natural resources. This situation has two aspects. On one hand, we can carry to great lengths our working out of the implications of the boundedness of human action at any historical moment, treating in a summary and highly simplified way the question of the nature and source of human modes of exploitation of this ultimate 'receptacle'. On the other hand, we can recognize that the human psyche is not simple, obvious, automatically well-informed and capable of performing in a moment calculations of unthinkable complexity. We can turn our attention from the *field* of action to the *source* of action. The theories we examined in Chapter VI go to an extreme length, not only in simplifying but in simplifying right out of existence the role of the human psyche in human affairs. In them the most subtle and elusive of all economic questions, the inducement to invest, is reduced to the Accelerator, the mechanical, proportionate relationship between size of flow of net investment and pace of growth of general output. Here Economic Man is reduced from omniscience to automatism. The contest between the *field* and the *source* for our attention cannot be resolved once for all by a single stroke or a finally general theory. It can be coped with only be a continuing dialectic, an endless resort to first one tool and then another. The ultimate riddle is not for us to solve but to administer.

INDEX

O

For EU product safety concerns, contact us at Calle de José Abascal, 56–1°,
28003 Madrid, Spain or eugpsr@cambridge.org.

www.ingramcontent.com/pod-product-compliance
Ingram Content Group UK Ltd.
Pitfield, Milton Keynes, MK11 3LW, UK
UKHW032214150325
456256UK00011B/202

* 9 7 8 0 5 2 1 1 4 7 5 5 2 *